Hannah Hauxwell

HANNAH'S STORY

W R Mitchell

GREAT NORTHERN

Great Northern Books

PO Box 213, Ilkley, LS29 9WS

www.greatnorthernbooks.co.uk

ISBN: 978 1 905080 41 0

Design and layout: David Burrill

Printed in China

CIP Data

A catalogue for this book is available from the British Library

CONTENTS

A CHRONOLOGY

1920s   –   Hannah's father buys Low Birk Hatt for £1,600.

1927   –   *August 1* – Birth of Hannah at Sleetburn, Baldersdale.

1940   –   Death of Grandma Elizabeth.

1941   –   Hannah leaves school.

1947   –   The grimmest spell of winter weather.

1958   –   Death of Lydia, Hannah's mother.

1961   –   Death of Hannah's uncle, leaving her alone at the farm.

1962   –   A winter memorable for its heavy snowfalls.

1973   -   *January 30* – Screening of *Too Long a Winter*.

1973   –   Publication of *Hannah in Yorkshire*.

1978   –   In a cruel winter, electricity lines blown down.

1980   –   Hannah invited to Buckingham Palace when the Queen Mother celebrates her 80th birthday.

1988   –   Another especially grim winter, Hannah decides to leave Low Birk Hatt.

1989   –   Publication of *Seasons of My Life: The Story of a Solitary Daleswoman*.

1993   –   Publication of *Hannah's North Country*.

1999   –   Great Northern publishes *Hannah Hauxwell: The Commonsense Book of a Countrywoman*.

PHOTO CREDITS

Fred Broomfield: Pages 104, 106
Rev L.M. Daniel: 56
Mike Kipling: 9, 15, 17, 22, 25, 39, 51, 58, 79, 155
W.R. Mitchell: 11, 44, 46, 48, 64, 66, 83, 88, 89, 90, 98, 99, 102, 108, 110, 112, 116 120, 123, 125, 127, 128, 131, 132, 134, 139, 141, 142, 147, 149, 158
Northern Echo: 30. 40, 76, 84, 94, 96, 117, 150, 152
North Yorkshire County Library: 6
Yorkshire Post Newspapers: 20, 54, 68, 81, 85, 92, 93
Yorkshire Television: 19, 26, 32, 33, 34, 42, 52, 60

Hannah Hauxwell and W R Mitchell, March 2008.

I am pleased with this book. I hope you like it. The book
began as one of several ideas in a discussion with David
Joy, who asked our mutual friend, Bill Mitchell, to write it.
Bill and his wife Freda were regular visitors to my farm.
The photographs were taken by many good friends.

Hannah Hauxwell

INTRODUCTION

I first became aware of Hannah Hauxwell on a January evening in 1973 when Yorkshire Television screened a film entitled *Too Long a Winter*. It was shot in monochrome at Low Birk Hatt, in Baldersdale, a valley that unfolds, endlessly it seems, to the west of Romaldkirk, beginning in the temperate zone of Teesdale and ending with the chilly moors of the high Pennines.

Teesdale, being the cradle of one of our major rivers and a botanist's delight, has achieved wide fame. Tourists stand, astonished, where the infant river goes milk-white as it descends a dolerite staircase at Cauldron Snout. Lower down, and even more spectacular, is High Force, where the river, in the early manhood of its life, tumbles some sixty feet from a lip of rock into a plunge pool.

Baldersdale, a geographic cul de sac, lies off the main tourist routes. The film I saw on that January evening was hardly likely to attract tourists, though it was an inspiration for about five million televiewers. They were seeing, in most cases for the first time, what farm life is like where a landscape and climate are a permanent test of the calibre of the residents, namely a few families long established on hill farms. Baldersdale is no area for weaklings.

The film, with no professional actors, had a backdrop in a sunless, wintry world, with the dalesfolk playing themselves. We saw the farmfolk scratting a living in little brown-stoned farmhouses and, elsewhere, Olive Field, the benevolent lady at the big house, Lartington Hall. Her first appearance was in a

Hannah Hauxwell, photographed at Low Birk Hatt Farm by Bertram Unné in 1966, well before she was 'discovered' by the media seven years later. She was wearing a 'Harding Apron', a garment made of sackcloth to cover ordinary clothes.

Dramatic light over Baldersdale, a land that lies off the main tourist routes and is no area for weaklings.

chauffeur-driven Rolls Royce. She was seen later as hostess to the dalefolk with feasting and dancing.

Before global warning became an urgent matter, the denizens of Baldersdale were tuned to a situation where nothing much grew until May and growth stopped about mid-September. On a hill farm, livestock is not reared for eating but for breeding. At a certain age, sheep are drafted from the hill farms to the lowlands, where they can put on weight and condition before entering the food chain.

Sheep did not have a place in the film *Too Long a Winter*. It was mostly about Hannah Hauxwell, a quiet-mannered, reflective, lonesome daleswoman living at a farm with the curious name of Low Birk Hatt and tending a small herd of cattle. Hannah, unlike other dale farmers, didn't fancy keeping sheep. Apart from anything else, she didn't care to handle greasy wool. Hannah was existing on 'next-to-nowt', as a local might say, summing up impoverishment. Each year, one of the half dozen 'beeasts' [cattle] was sold to augment Hannah's otherwise meagre income from letting out spare land.

Hannah, bobbing in and out of the film, was a star who wore careworn clothes. Yet her bright appearance, her gentle manner, her wisdom and her persistency in the face of grim natural obstacles, at around the 900-ft contour line, were an inspiration for urban-based televiewers. Barry Cockcroft, the producer, gave us a lot of muck, murk and misery.

In a turbulent world, Hannah was at peace with herself. After she had worked hard, she revelled in intangibles such as the play of light on familiar views. Indoors, lacking all mod-cons, she nurtured the spiritual aspects of life by reading the Good Book and playing hymns on a harmonium that had belonged to her mother. Somebody who did not like its wheezy sound called the harmonium "an ill wind that nobody blows any good". Hannah listened to *The Archers* on her battery-operated radio until the story line – like much else offered to the public – took a nose-dive in morality. Luxury to Hannah was supping tea from a mug before a coal fire.

Low Birk Hatt and its associated byre looked down on Hury reservoir (curious name), one of a trio of reservoirs that, with an irregular shoreline, were picturesque, not to simply be regarded as a gigantic reserve of cold water. In the film the sky was almost invariably mucky, being grey, at times even black. A high Pennine winter, harsh and protracted, kept layers of snow on fields and ridges. Now and again, the clouds parted to let a ray of sunlight – as intense as a searchlight beam – reach the frozen earth.

The dalesfolk, restricting themselves to a few essential jobs, kept warm as best

Low Birk Hatt Farm. Hannah was brought here at the age of three and knew no other life for the next fifty-plus years.

they could. Cattle rarely lowed. Sheep bleated for a bit o' fodder. Hannah's tiny herd of cattle, ensconced in the byre, dined on sweet-smelling hay and what water Hannah had the strength to carry in buckets from a stream fifty yards from home.

The stream tended to dry up in summer heat and was crusted with ice in deepest winter. Hannah had a long rod with which to break up the ice. Hannah's strenuous efforts at water collecting dominated the opening sequence of the film. Tending stock was her principal occupation. Life was primitive, especially at milking time in summer, when – carrying pail and three-legged stool – she pursued one of her cows around a field, then persuaded it to settle down and part with its milk.

Hannah Bayles Tallentire Hauxwell, to use her Sunday name, had for many years lived in what a visiting journalist called "solitary confinement". She was also

described as "a mountain hermit". Hannah, brought to Low Birk Hatt at the age of three years, had known no other life. She grew up in the 1930s, which economically were grim, with more sobs than laughter. The family consisted of parents, grandparents and two elderly uncles.

Hannah's mother, Lydia, small and plump – not unlike Queen Victoria – had scarcely time to stop and scratch her back. With a large family and only three bedrooms, sleeping space was at a premium. Hannah and her parents slept in one bed. A luckless uncle had set his bed under the stairs. Hannah was the only child, having no handy playmates. Her nearest young friend lived over a mile away. A shy girl, Hannah did not care much for school and left when she attained her fourteenth birthday.

The film *Too Long a Winter* appealed to me because it did not romanticise the life of a dale-country women. Hannah, this "lady of the hills", to quote from yet another newspaper account, was not yet 50 years of age and leading a solitary existence in a remote setting, exposed to cutting winds. Domestically, she bathed using a cow pail. She had an earth closet and washed in a poss-tub. Her monthly food bill with the grocer (who left the groceries, including some cheese and a tin of Spam, on a wall-top a mile or so from her home) rose to an unsustainable £5. Holidays were something she looked forward to, hoping each year for a three-day break with relatives at Mickleton.

The communal treat at the Hall was welcome, though Hannah, on film, looked wistful. At home, she was quietly forbearing as she coped with drudgery. All this delighted the film-makers. They had found a spirited, characterful woman who was happy just being herself. Though quiet of manner and soft of speech, Hannah radiated faith, pride in her ancestors and love towards her native dale. She was unfazed when a television camera was trained upon her.

Hannah might shudder and shiver in winter, as the snow-dogs howled, but she gloried in the Pennine springtime. Then cock tewits (lapwings), displaying to their admiring mates, tumbled in the air, rising again on tufty wings when it seemed likely they would dash themselves against the ground. Lapwings nested in a shallow depression among the rush-bobs not far from home. Curlews uttered their fluty refrains as, having climbed steeply, they went into a long glide over their

Hannah Hauxwell, photographed at the time of her 'discovery' in 1973.

The purplish tinge that gives the Teesdale moors a special beauty in late summer.

nesting territories. Thorn trees displayed a mass of white blossom but creaked and wheezed in the wind like asthmatic old men.

In summer, a low-slung moon shone on the reservoir that lapped and fretted below her home.

In retrospect, the peak of the year seemed little more than a blink between two long winters. It tended to be dull and moist. As grass grew lustily, in unaccustomed warmth, horse-flies, known as clegs, sent the cows into a frenzy of movement known to the dalesfolk as *gadding*. For Hannah, happiness was tinged with the sadness, knowing that nature's clock did not stop.

Late summer had its special beauty – a purplish tinge on the moors. She never really knew what lay beyond them until 1993, when she was taken to some of Yorkshire's most scenic places for the book *Hannah's North Country*. Her first visit to High Force preceded this period. On a Saturday after the Second World War, when Hannah was in her twenties, and staying with Cousin Norman and his wife Lizzie, she observed the wondrous waterfall. She commented: "I doubt whether mother or father ever saw High Force; they never mentioned it."

In autumn, the dale was adorned with its Jacob's coat of many colours. Then the lean forefinger of winter pricked the summer bubble. When the lapwings were flocking on low ground and curlews had drifted away to the coast, the gabbling of Canada geese on the nearby reservoir infused life into an otherwise quiet world. Our lady of the hills prepared for another long winter. To step outside the house at night was to walk under an arc of stars or into darkness. Pinpricks of light indicated where other farmsteads lay. It was quiet except for the occasional barking of a farm dog.

In winter, updale families seemed to grow an extra skin. Hannah kept warm through hard work. Going to bed was a cheerless experience. The temperature in an unheated bedroom remained low. Frost pictures appeared on bedroom windows overnight. Said Hannah: "I am very lonely in the winter. Some of the winters have been so bad that I don't want to think about them... If I have enough stock in I can see the winter out all right. But if the bad weather lasts too long, neighbouring farmers help me out...It isn't an easy life but I am used to it. I could have left years ago, but it would not be easy to move away. I am very attached to the place."

The wondrous waterfall of High Force, where the River Tees tumbles some sixty feet from a lip of rock into a plunge pool.

Hannah was greatly attached to her sheepdog – a constant companion and invaluable help at Low Birk Hatt.

Tim, the Jack Russell which provided much-needed solace after the move down to Cotherstone.

She was also attached to her sheepdog Uffa who, alas, had to be "put down" in 1985. Tim, a Jack Russell, helped to fill an empty place in her heart when she retired to Cotherstone. Tim was "first on the list" as she rose. He took precedence over breakfast, re-established his bond with Hannah by settling down on her knee – known to Hannah as a "sitting" - before being taken for a morning walk. "We go out in all kinds of weather. It doesn't worry me. I'm used to it." Invariably, Hannah dons wellingtons, "my everlasting friends".

DALE COUNTRY

The home-dale of Hannah Hauxwell lies to the east of the Pennines. It is a shallow valley, a cul de sac for wheeled traffic. Any outcropping rock is a warm brown gritstone. The highest farm, aptly named Balder Head, lies near one of a trio of reservoirs with water lapping up to the garden wall. In 1974, the Boundary Commissioners switched the area from Yorkshire into County Durham. Not that this made much difference to the outlook and local culture. Once the road on the north side of the valley continued beyond Balder Head in a green track leading to Brough in Westmorland. The moor has reclaimed it. To go further, one must have a horse or wear good boots. Ramsden wrote: "There are no houses or trees on this moorland crossing, but it is saved from monotony by the distant views of the Mickle Fell Range and the final, sudden outlook over the Eden Valley."

Hannah's birthplace lay a dozen miles from the market town of Barnard Castle, which I first visited in 1962, when the place was bursting at the seams and Lord Barnard resided in magnificent Raby Castle. The town was named after the castle that Bernard Baliol built in the 12th century. Everyone knew the place as "Barney". I jostled with folk in the Wednesday market, a custom almost as old as the town, attracting villagers and farming families from miles around, though no longer did womenfolk sit round the elaborate Market Cross with their baskets of butter, eggs and cheese.

Hannah's world was, in contrast with the bustle in Barney, a shallow dale bounded by ranges of fells. To her, the world beyond was something people only talked about. Early in the nineteenth century J E Buckrose, author of *Rambles in the North Yorkshire Dales*, visited Baldersdale, attracted by the Fairy Cupboards and the river bridge. "It is possible to ascend the parapet of Balder Bridge by stone steps, and thus obtain a charming view of the river and the old mill, no longer in

The elaborate Market Cross at Barnard Castle, where womenfolk once gathered from miles around to sell butter, eggs and cheese.

use. Beyond the mill, the river Balder breaks joyously into a series of cascades which flash and sing in the sunset."

J Fairfax-Blakeborough, who wrote copiously about rural Yorkshire, had never heard of Baldersdale until a member of the Ramblers' Association told him it was "up Barnard Castle way". Fairfax-Blakeborough, determined to see the dale for himself, chatted with the Fawcett family, flockmasters and amateur musicians. Each member played a musical instrument and so provided an orchestra within one household. "I gather there is a Wesleyan Chapel in Baldersdale, so the couplet applied to Bonfield Ghyll, 'where the Lord never was, and never will', does not apply."

Douglas M Ramsden, writing in 1946, when dale-life was sustained largely by the native born, wrote of the River Balder that it "pours its brown, peaty water, gathered from the bogs and mosses north of Stainmore, into the Tees at Cotherstone". This was the village to which Hannah would eventually retire from farming. When Ramsden wrote, the aforementioned mill was still standing by "the choked mill-race" which "leads to the skeleton of an undershot wheel that is still connected and geared to the grinding mechanism inside the walls".

Ramsden added: "Reservoirs, with their unnatural shore-lines, do not always merge fittingly in their landscapes, but in this instance they do succeed in adding an element of interest to the bleak basin of Upper Baldersdale. There are few trees here, apart from the clumps acting as windbreaks to the scattered farms. The bare fields slope gently on either side of the valley to the moorland rims... These hills have been preserved from erosion and the planing of the ice by their hard, gritstone caps."

Lydia Hauxwell, the mother of Hannah, was to be seen in a photograph with a calm contented face that belied the toil and worries of the depression years. Life was always hard for the Hauxwells. Hannah developed a pride not only in the Baldersdale of today but in its past, tales of which were recounted by the older end. It was once home to a few hundred people and in addition to the small mill there were two inns. Hannah's great grandfather, with horse and cart, collected butter and eggs from the farms and sold them in Barnard Castle.

An anonymous contributor to *The Dalesman* in the summer of 1977 commented that Hannah must represent the last of her day and generation still living in some of the spartan conditions relating to farming life. "I lived my early life in Upper Teesdale. My grandfather and mother were born at Baillie Hill Farm, on the other side of the moor away from the great reservoir across which the keenest, bleakest winds sweep towards Hannah's farm...I am older than Hannah

and I know all about life on a small farm in the early 1900s."

Furniture in the farmsteads was plain and comfortless. Oil lamps gave poor lighting. There was a black cast-iron range whose fire provided heat for the room, for cooking to provide warm water. Logs were inserted for extra and quick heat when baking. The stone-flagged floor would have some "clipped" rugs covering part of it. All water had to be carried into the house – and out again after use. The land supplied most of the food that was wrested from it in arduous, endless toil with nature. In winter, the hardy freshness of the air and the bleakness of the winds spurred the workers on to get their outside jobs done quickly in winter.

Food consisted of rabbits, hares, gamebirds, bacon, lard, butter, eggs, milk, potatoes and vegetables. Soft fruits would be grown also – raspberries and gooseberries, with blackberries and bilberries to be found beside or on the moors.

Romaldkirk, the Teesdale village that forms one of the gateways to Baldersdale.

Stores of white and brown flour were kept in a divided chest. Not less than one stone of flour was baked into bread once or twice a week, also a large quantity of teacakes. A grocer called at the farms for orders once a month. He later delivered flour, oatmeal, cheese, rice, sugar, salt, currants, treacle and items for curing bacon.

"I think I have had the best of two worlds, for it has been my good fortune to live in Upper Teesdale and later in York. But at seventy I still wish I could visit Romaldkirk more often to relive those happy youthful days, when the moors, valleys and rivers of Upper Teesdale made a kingdom of our own, which my sisters and I never tired of exploring." Hannah grew up on a farm which cost her father £1,600. He was repaying the money, with difficulty, in the form of mortgages. When father died of pernicious anaemia, mother contrived to meet the mortgage repayments; she must also care for four elderly folk.

HANNAH DISCOVERED

Good fortune did not attend Hannah. When in post-war days, a North Pennine organisation was set up to help farm folk attune themselves to changing conditions, she was referred to – though not by name – as a woman who ran a farm single-handed and contrived to live on about £170 a year. Alec Donaldson, of the *Yorkshire Post*, intrigued when he learnt that Hannah subsisted on an average of £3 a week, tracked her down to the eighty-acre Low Birk Hatt Farm, "deep in the quiet confines of Baldersdale".

Hannah described her holding as thirty-seven acres of meadow and forty-three acres of "much rougher ground". Donaldson noted that "its limited acres make up a little world of last year's spent grasses, powdered snow, and a cold wind which soughs or shrieks according to mood". Hannah looked "very feminine in her masculine clothes". Her life had been hard, yet she had a smooth pink and white face. "Her hair was greying, her work-grimed hands are fine and sensitive."

The visiting journalist noted that Hannah had "a curious but-not-of-this-century grace and courtesy of speech and manner...She shows a woman's concern for the ritual of tea-making and serving, despite her old Harris tweed jacket, her breeches and gum boots." In the house, there was no electricity, no gas. Water, as mentioned earlier, was drawn from a fickle stream not too far from the house. Paraffin lamps provided the illumination on dark winter days. Coal and wood fed the living room fire. It turned out that the only time she saw a newspaper was

Hannah drawing water from the 'fickle stream' shortly after she was 'discovered' by Alec Donaldson of the Yorkshire Post.

when it was left by a visiting friend. Her radio set did not work at the time of the journalist's visit.

Neighbours were few. Hannah, having had no other home, liked the countryside, the privacy and the freedom. She had to walk three fields distance to a gate where her bread was left. She walked more fields to High Birk Hatt, where her groceries were delivered, being kept for her by good neighbours. She had been out of the dale only five times in the previous year.

Her mother had died in 1958 and the uncle, who had lived with them, "passed away" three years later. Hannah, left alone with the farm and "its sour acres", realised she could not farm Low Birk Hatt on the old-time scale. She sold off the thirty or so dairy cattle, letting the allotment land to neighbours for sheep grazing and the in-bye land for summer-feeding cattle. Her limited income was derived from the land-letting. She kept three or four head of cattle which she wintered indoors.

Alec Donaldson was aware that Low Birk Hatt, though solitary, "stands hard on the Pennine Way and by May she might expect its very attenuated traffic to start. She looks forward to them and is patently flattered when people greet her with a 'We saw you last year and wondered how you were getting along'." Alec met Hannah on a day of bitter cold; she had spoken wistfully and hopefully of summer. "Ah, then it is really beautiful." She could not wish to have a better place "when the days are long and the air is warm... Oh, yes, when May comes the grip of loneliness on Low Birk Hatt is eased – reluctantly and almost imperceptibly."

In summer, she could go around the farm repairing stone walls, putting in stakes where they were needed and spreading muck. "Then this lonely, independent woman who has no brothers or sisters or other near relatives can look forward to visitors other than the postman and her other few callers..." Hannah had talked animatedly to her journalistic visitor about the time, two years before when, rather poorly, she was conveyed to Northallerton hospital. The staff and other patients were "very, very kind".

Her eyes had lit up with the recollection of that intimate contact with other humans in a close community. At home, she might go for as much as ten days without speaking to another soul. If she had been taken ill on the morrow, she might lie unaided for days. "It's a chance I have to take," she would say, calmly. She had a few pleasures besides her work. Reading was one, although this was becoming a restricted pleasure because of eye pains. "She loves the birds around her home: the swans, geese and ducks on the reservoir below, the curlews which bubble on the high land around her and the owls which screech about the house...

And she enjoys playing the harmonium ('I play simple things for my own entertainment') which has a prominent place in her living kitchen."

Was her life to be recommended to others? "She ponders and thinks, just as she does over every question. Then with a politeness which is unexpected because it is so unusual, replies: 'I think perhaps it is not to be recommended. It is too extreme. My income is very little, and I try hard to keep outgoings to £150. It is not adequate and barely provides for the necessities of life...I suppose there is a happy medium. It would, I think, be nicer to see rather more people and hear something of what is going on in the world'."

SAYINGS OF HANNAH

The old house and me will stay together for as long as we can.

I wish it was always summer.

Only the weeds seem to thrive; it's amazing how they recover after a bad winter.

I'm not cut out to be in any other place.

Wellingtons – my everlasting friends.

FIVE MILLION FANS

Hannah was propelled into national fame on January 30, 1973, when Yorkshire Television, having seen the article, turned the theme into a documentary, *Too Long a Winter*. Shown on a winter evening, it impressed because of its realism. Nothing quite like it had appeared on television. The lonesome lady of Low Birk Hatt was someone special. Her white hair and tattered clothes contrasted with her rosy complexion. It was as if someone had splashed cold water on her face, stimulating capillary action.

The viewer ached for her as she was seen struggling through snow to find some open water on the stream that normally flowed some 50 yards from home but which, in deepest winter, had a crust of ice. Her debut in a blizzard sequence showed her, bent with effort, hanging on to the end of a rope as she virtually dragged one of her animals on the first stage of a journey to the next farm. The journey would end, as far as Hannah was concerned, with its sale at the local auction mart.

There was also a sequence of socialising at Lartington Hall, which – in contrast with Hannah's farm – was palatial, built in the reign of Charles I and occupied by an important Catholic family of the Maires, the last descendant dying here in 1897. The cameraman, Mostafa Hammuri, filmed at the extremes of exposure, coping as well with the glare of new snow as with the gloom of a winter afternoon. It was appropriate for him to secure some fine sequences in which the

Hannah – as portrayed in the Northern Echo on the day
following the transmission of Too Long a Winter.

Two 'stills' taken during the filming of Too Long a Winter.
Above: In front of Low Birk Hatt. In the background are Hury Reservoir
and the distinguished white cow 'Her Ladyship'.
Opposite page: Hanging out washing behind the farm.

sun set over water. Hannah was particularly fond of the reflection of a full moon on a shimmering reservoir.

A Wolverhampton reader of *The Dalesman* wrote: "I thank her through your magazine for taking us into her home and, in days of slick presentation and over-emphasis of material things, for giving us a lucid and genuine account of her day-to-day activities." Details of her spartan way of life were irresistible to those who, by comparison, lived luxurious lives. They were captivated by life at Low Birk Hatt, where survival depended on letting out fields for her neighbours' sheep and selling the odd cow.

Horses did the heavy work, being harnessed to a cart or, in difficult terrain, to a joiner-made wooden sled that ran easily over the springy grass when it was being used at haytime. Hannah was to recall: "We had several horses at the farm down the years." Short, sharp names were preferred. She had special memories of Snip, the mare; of Dick, "a nice little chap"; of Prince and Blossom, the last-named being a miniature Clydesdale which, alas, developed a heart condition and had to be put down.

Some farmers were especially good at "brekking in stags", young, unbroken horses of about 15 hands. Known as "gallowa's", they were good at any heavy job. From March to July, the main mating season for horses, the dale-country was traversed by men leading be-ribboned entire stallions from farm to farm to serve the mares. Few people saw a horse drop its foal. It was the shortest birth process imaginable. A farmer would arise in the morning and discover that the expected foal had been born and was standing, albeit, a little shakily, on its stilt-like legs.

A farm horse that spent much of the early summer on rough pastureland was given additional feed at the approach of haytime. Oats and bran put the sheen back on its coat and a sparkle into its eye. Then the farmer took it to the nearest smith for its pre-haytime shoeing. A good horse had a working life spanning some twenty years. Other horses "got done soon on" and were taken to the knacker's yard.

Hannah's cows – big gentle beasts, chestnut and white – were virtually pets, with names like Pickaboo and Rosa. The last-named was a daughter of a white cow given the distinguished name of Her Ladyship. Rosa kept Hannah warm during a particularly hard winter. In the evening, she would draw from Rosa some warm

'Her Ladyship', with whom Hannah had an enduring love-hate relationship.

milk, then settle down in the byre to spend the night using Rosa as a hot water bottle. At times, Hannah's cattle became too familiar and a young beast ventured into the farmhouse. It was Hannah's fault; she had accidentally left open a field gate and also the back door of the farmhouse. Returning home, she found the animal had walked through the kitchen into the living room. There was no space for it to turn round. The animal solved its own problem – by reversing.

In the old days, new-calved cows were kept near the farm and fed large quantities of oatmeal gruel, into which some linseed might be mixed to give them "a bit o' heat". A farmer dreaded the day when a cow aborted its calf or showed symptoms of John's disease, "a desperate thing". In pre-James Herriot days, milk fever was cured by pumping oxygen into the cow's bag. Linseed oil or castor oil was used when there was a "stoppage". Ringworm was overspread with a mixture of engine oil and black sulphur. Or collop [bacon] fat and brimstone – "wi' a bit o' turpentine".

It was not unusual to milk cattle out-of-doors, transporting the milk to the farm buildings in a back-can, a metal container for milk with a harness which might be slipped over the shoulder. Inside the back-can was a baffle so the milk would not "slop about" when it was being borne to the farm. When not in use, the milking stool might be placed in a tree, "where it wouldn't get wet and mucky". Cows were frisky when first overwintered in a byre. A dog was needed to round them up. Then they fell into the milking routine and knew their places. A handful of special feed in a bucket encouraged them to drop their milk. The milker, having attended to one cow, would turn to see another, standing patiently, "watchin' t'bucket, wi'slather running over her chin".

Unlike Hannah, who made pets of her stock and parted with them, one at a time, with regret, dale-country farmers tended to dispose of them when they had their third or fourth calf. You might conceal the age of a cow by removing some of the rings that formed on the horns with the passing years. An unscrupulous chap would file the horn to take the wrinkles out. Today, he would have been done for jiggery-pokery.

TRIPS TO LONDON

The screening of the first film created an avalanche of gifts, letters, food parcels and well-meaning offers. Hannah continued to live her life unchanged. She featured in a book, *Hannah in Yorkshire* (soon to be reprinted in a new form by *Dalesman*). Stardom led to visits to London. She attended a Women of the Year Luncheon at a posh hotel and was subsequently one of many guests at a Royal Garden Party in the grounds of Buckingham Palace.

Leaving her cattle to be cared for by trusted neighbours, Hannah stayed the previous night at the home of friends in Barnard Castle. "I'd had a bit of a day, that day, so I went in my old clothes. I had a lovely bath – a luxury – and next morning a cup of tea, served when I was still in bed." Now in her best setting-off clothes, and receiving every kindness and consideration from her friends, she was driven to London.

I subsequently asked Hannah what she had for tea at the event held in the Buckingham Palace grounds. She replied: "Brown bread and butter, which I would have had at home. I love brown bread. And a lovely little pancake, a cheese scone, a piece of fruit cake and a piece of chocolate cake. Being me, I had two cups of tea." She had been delighted to hear a band play 'Roses of the South', a favourite piece.

Hannah had never been close enough to see the faces of the Queen and Queen Mother. "When they set off on their walk, they went in the opposite direction. I did

Over: The bridge at Barnard Castle, the nearest town to Baldersdale. It was from here that Hannah set off on many of her memorable visits to places far afield.

*Unfamiliar luxury in a central London hotel,
with 'Big Ben' just visible in the distance.*

notice they were both in blue, the Queen Mother in her paler blue. It was rather a nice experience to hear the National Anthem played in the Queen's presence." After the Garden Party, she stayed overnight at a London hotel, returning north by train on the following day. A taxi conveyed her from Darlington to her remote home. "I should think I would be home just after four," she recalled, still with a sense of wonderment.

Another trip was to Malhamdale Show, held beside the little greystone village, with a backdrop composed of the Cove, a sheer limestone cliff, contrasting markedly with the low horizons of her native Baldersdale. Hannah, having agreed to be the chief guest, was collected by car. John Geldard, the local farmer, who performed this duty, had the inevitable wait for this "late getter-up". At the showfield, Hannah attracted more attention than the livestock. A queue of people who had bought her book waited patiently for her signature. Hannah was not to be rushed. She painstakingly wrote her name and added the date. She charmed everyone at the show luncheon – by being herself.

HOME PLEASURES

At Low Birk Hatt, a power failure would put her on short rations – a cold drink and some corned beef, with another cold drink before bedtime. She had food, but the effort of coping with the cattle in grim weather left her little energy to care for herself. For years, a coal fire had been out of the question. The chimneys were in need of attention. After one protracted power cut, she was alerted to the resumption of power when, transporting manure to a heap in the winter gloom, there was a sudden blaze of light at a farm up the hillside. Switching on the power at Low Birk Hatt, she thankfully turned to the electric kettle, which in the cold snap had developed a layer of ice. Slowly, heat returned to the rooms and made life bearable.

Groceries delivered from Cotherstone were set down at a point within easy walking distance of the farm. The monthly delivery was, thankfully, not curtailed in snowtime. Hannah had a basic food stock – potatoes and "tins and things" – and was fond of imported items like butter and cheese. A milk kit, in a permanent place near the dale road, served various purposes. At times it was a repository for workaday clothes when she changed to wear something more suited to social events.

With the death of mother and uncle, Hannah was alone, a state she could never remember, having been brought to Low Birk Hatt at the age of three. Loneliness is a state of mind. There was much at the farm to remind her of family and friends. She had the companionship of a sprightly dog named Chip and two cats. The needs of several cattle kept her occupied for most of the daylight hours. Sheep had never been her prime money-maker.

Indoors, she passed most of the long winter in reading by the light of a paraffin lamp. The Bible was a major source of inspiration. She also had her copies

In the days before mains electricity reached Low Birk Hatt, Hannah passed most of the long winter in reading by the light of a paraffin lamp.

of *The Dalesman* close to hand. A battery-operated radio kept her in touch with world events. She had inherited a harmonium from her mother, who had been a talented musician. This instrument, seen elsewhere, was described by a wincing hearer as "an ill wind that nobody blows any good".

On a visit to the farm when the day was chilly and wet (looking, as an old farmer said, "as though it had bin up aw neet"), Freda and I had no response to our knocking on the back door. Then we heard the squeal of a cord window being opened. Hannah looked out from her bedroom, remarking: "It's one of my off days." A pause. "It's a pity about Russell Harty." The television personality had died that morning. At least, the radio was working.

On our first visit we had noticed that the huge fireplace was blocked off, which was a pity. Old farms need the open fireplace if only to ensure there is a draught to keep the place dry. We detected a dampness in the air, even though a tiny electric fire tried valiantly to keep the large room warm. We saw a paraffin lamp, which reminded me of my own courtship, and especially the first time I was invited to the farm for "Sunday tea". Part way through the meal, the paraffin lamp went out. There was an interlude while the lamp-glass was washed, the wick trimmed and the lamp re-lit. It was a comon experience.

Hannah's living room had two framed photographs – one of Granny and another of a military gentleman whose identity had been forgotten. Mother had said she resembled Grandad, so she was left in place. And there were two majestic long-case clocks which, having been made in Barnard Castle, had travelled only six miles in their long lives.

Hannah recalled her mother with great affection. When father died, she had had been left in charge of some elderly folk who were sick. Consequently, she had many sleepless nights. Her loving mother was a marvellous companion. "She was the great one in my life…" Our experience of Low Birk Hatt was restricted to the kitchen and living room. Rumour had it that Hannah slept in a four-poster bed, without curtains, which on many such beds were drawn at night, retaining heat and banishing draughts. In winter, little time was lost in undressing and donning night attire. Hannah liked a good weight of bedspreads.

VISITORS TO THE FARM

Freda, my wife – a farmer's daughter – and I first met Hannah on a Bank Holiday when, keen to escape the tourist throng, we motored from our home at Giggleswick, travelling against the grain of the country to an Empty Quarter – the North Pennines – where farmfolk are thinly spread. From Hawes we crossed the Buttertubs Pass to Swaledale, stopping briefly to peer into one of the potholes and reminding ourselves of the story of a local man who, when asked about the depth of one pothole, replied: "It's bottomless. And if you come over here I'll show you one that's deeper still." From just beyond Keld we took the steep zig-zag road leading to West Stonesdale and an unfenced road through sheep country to Tan Hill. Thence into Arkengarthdale, with another steepish ascent and descent into Hannah Hauxwell Country. Our entry into Baldersdale, a lile offshoot of Teesdale, was via Romaldkirk. Being vaguely aware of the location of Low Birk Hatt, we parked the car near one of the big reservoirs and trudged across rough pastureland, picking our way between the rush-bobs to where a track, straight as a bowshot, led to an iron gate. Beyond, hopefully, was the farmhouse – and Hannah. We had a quiet confidence that she would be at home.

We espied Low Birk Hatt from afar. It stood on the near side of a sparkling reservoir which, we gathered, was Hannah's reserve water supply and a place where, if the native stream dried up, she might surreptitiously wash her clothes. We carried a freshly-baked cake – two layers of sponge, with raspberry jam in

Opposite and over: Hannah, photographed by the author during his many visits to Low Birk Hatt.

between. Surely, no more delicate object had been carried on the broad track which rose grandly to an iron gate.

In this gritstone country, the outbuildings at Low Birk Hatt were tonally brown, contrasting with the limestone grey of our own district in the west. We noticed a few dislodged slates and a muck-heap substantial enough to qualify for the attention of the Ordnance Survey. As we knocked at the back door of the farmstead, Hannah's dog – named Chip – began a noisy round of barking. The door opened. Before us, in real life rather than on film, stood Hannah, who had coaxed Chip into another room and shut the door. Her head was crowned by wispy white hair. Her ruddy face held a serene expression. Her clothes were well-worn, to say the least. She wore trousers and had donned wellies. Beyond the little kitchen lay a spacious living space that was in 'a scrow' [it was untidy] mainly because Hannah had not found the time or energy for rigorous house-keeping.

In that summer of 1978, Hannah was a "home bird", living with new-fangled electricity but, despite the near presence of a reservoir, beyond the reach of piped water and dependent on the local beck for her supply. The beck dried up periodically and, in winter, was plated with ice. Hannah had scanned the account books kept by her father and wondered how he managed to keep the farm viable. "It was never a milking place, being too far from the road. We bred stock. We sold a new-calved beast or two. Or perhaps a heifer going for store. We also sold bullocks. And a few sheep..."

On that first visit, we sat – where we could find a seat - in a large, gloriously cluttered room, the clutter including heaps of parcels (presumably from well-wishers), secured by binder twine. I admired the long-case clocks. A strand of binder twine, neatly tied with a bow, was to be seen around one of the clocks. (Years later, during a programme called *Through the Keyhole*, when a panel was asked to guess the home of a celebrity from pictures of its contents, I would instantly recognise Hannah's abode – by the binder twine round the clock).

In 1980, when I made a particularly detailed note of our visit, she reported it had been late when she turned the cattle out of the byres on to fresh grass. She had been "a bit tired this last week or two. By the time I got through the milking I had had enough." A pause. "In summer I live; in winter, I exist." Mercifully, the previous winter had not been too bad, though with one or two snowy days. She had to trudge through snow for a supply of bread and returned home exhausted, with wet clothes to change, a meal to make and the cattle to be fed and milked. Happily, as the work got under way, the snowfall stopped and the wind settled. (On holiday, Freda and I usually selected a picture postcard for Hannah with a

special feature – a cloudless blue sky).

Images from the television film remained in my mind. I repeatedly saw her tugging a recalcitrant cow through drifted snow. I shivered as she slithered through snow to fill a pan with water from the local stream. Norman Swallow, a well-known north-country broadcaster, dubbed the film a classic and observed: "In addition to the marvellous scenery, which for me brought back nostalgic memories, I thrilled to the simple tastes and cheerful philosophy of these people."

Trade was not always good. "Mother, like me, wasn't a business woman. She did not like to do it. Grandmother was much better at selling things." Hannah had little time for sheep. "They can be mischievous. And there are things I can't do with them." The Hauxwells' sheep were driven to a nearby farm, owned by the Fawcetts, to be dipped. Hannah didn't care to clip sheep but was happy to roll up the fleeces and put them in the wool sack.

As her eyesight began to fail, she found solace in listing to her radio. She kept a stable lamp handy in case there were power cuts. When she retired to bed, she swaddled herself in clothes, as well as blankets. A good bed cover was an old Army greatcoat that belonged to an uncle. Running a farm of 80-acres, albeit with comparatively little stock, made continuous physical demands on her.

Hannah remembered the hard graft of old-time haymaking with fork and rake. Eventually, a neighbour had baled the hay for her. If there was insufficient room in the outbuildings to hold the hay that had been mown, she stored the excess in a separate building, a good way from the farmhouse, using this outlying hay first. At times of snow or hard frost, she would transport bales to the shippon on a hand-hauled sled.

Summertime visitors included Kit Calvert, of Hawes, a great Dales character who first visited Hannah at Low Birk Hatt in 1973. Hannah enjoyed Kit's company and his stock of Wensleydale tales. Kit, like Hannah, had a rock-hard religious faith, with a tendency to hark back to the old days of chapel-going. Kit translated parts of the Bible into Dales dialect. When someone complained about his use of dialect, he pointed out that Jesus spoke in dialect; it was certainly not standard English. Here is Kit's rendering of the 23rd Psalm:

With Freda Mitchell – a farmer's daughter – on the occasion of the first meeting.

The gritstone country of Baldersdale, part of the 'Empty Quarter' of the North Pennines, where farmfolk are thinly spread.

The Lord is my Shipperd
Ah'll want fer nowt.
He lets m'bassock i' t'best pastur an taks mi'
Bi' t'watter side whar o's wyet on peeaceful.
He uplifts mi sould, an' maks things seea easy 'at
Ah can dew what's reet an' Gloryfy His neeame.
Even if ah git t'deeaths deeursteead ah's nut be freetened,
For he'll bi wi' mi.
His cruek an' esh plant 'll up hod mi,
Thoo puts a good meal afoor mi,
Reet anenst them' at upbraids mi,
Thou ceuls mi 'heead wi' oil.
An Ah've meeat an' drink t'spar.
Seurlie Thi goodness an' mercy 'al bi mine
Fer o't days o' mi life
And Ah'll beleng t' t'hoose o' the Lord fer ever.

The visit was recalled, in talks given to many church groups, by one of his companions on that day. He was the Rev L M Daniel, Rector of Bangor-on-Dee, who died in 1984, which was the same year as the death of Kit. His wife, using her husband's notes, wrote that – like the wine at the Wedding Feast at Canaan – the last day was quite the best. Having watched with intense interest and enjoyment the television programme *Too Long a Winter*, which portrayed the life of Hannah Hauxwell, we were delighted to find that Kit knew her. He needed no persuasion to pay her a visit.

The little party reached Baldersdale without confusion, "but it took us a little time to find Low Birk Hatt. Arriving unannounced we at first thought the place was deserted, and we had difficulty in finding the door due to a tall hedge of nettles. Eventually, we found Hannah at the back of the house where she was busily engaged in cleaning the calf-stall. She dropped tools at our approach, giving us such a wonderful welcome and insisting on taking us into the house.

"On entering, we went through the kitchen into the parlour. Never had we

Opposite: Using the 'new-fangled electricity' to catch up with fan mail.
Most of it remained unanswered as she simply did not have the time.

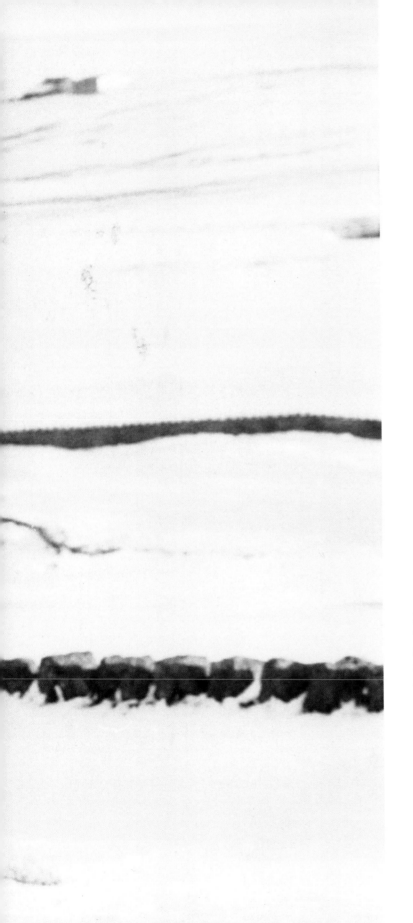

Hannah during one of the many winters that lived up to the film title and were truly too long. Trudging through snow to feed stock and obtain supplies could be exhausting.

Over: Summertime visitors to Low Birk Hatt included Kit Calvert, a great Dales character who shared with Hannah a rock-hard religious faith. A photograph was taken of the two of them arm-in-arm on a flagged path beside the farmhouse, with Hannah holding what was probably a muck fork.

seen so many meal bags inside a house. They were used for many purposes – one chair was padded with them. The table was piled high with gifts; there were boxes of biscuits and chocolates, new wellingtons, various garments, also a television set, electric lamps and an electric stove. We had the impression that though she greatly appreciated the kindness of the donors, these sophisticated gifts seemed meaningless to her."

These Yorkshire visitors were delighted by Hannah's turn of phrase and quick humour. "All too soon it was time to take our leave. With her gentle courtesy, Hannah accompanied us to the gate and we bade adieu to this country lady and her cow, Her Ladyship." A photograph was taken of Kit and Hannah arm-in-arm, on a flagged path beside the farmhouse. A smiling Hannah had in one hand a garden fork (or might it be a muck fork?). There were, of course, wellies on her feet.

SAYINGS OF HANNAH

I'm always late – and I'm no good at rushing.

If it wasn't for television, I'd have been unknown.

I like trousers; they are handy and comfortable.

Of marriage: There was no one really special in that line.

If you haven't had the bad, you can't appreciate the good.

You can't be a good farmer on a shoestring.

Hannah did not have much to do with sheep, but revelled in sounds drifting
in from nearby farms. This solitary ewe was photographed on Langdon
Common at the head of Teesdale.

LAMBING TIME

As mentioned, Hannah did not have much to do with sheep. She was "not up to sheeply jobs". But each spring, she revelled in sounds drifting in from sheep farms round about, notably the contralto voices of the ewes and the soprano arias of new-born lambs. On a hill farm, such as was to be found in Baldersdale, when tupping time arrived nature was allowed to take her course. If all the sheep did not lamb, it did not matter too much. Rearing twins in the upper dale-country was a chancy business.

Heavily pregnant ewes were taken off the moor or common and quartered in crofts near the farmhouse, where they might be inspected several times a day or even during the night if the weather was grim, the farmer cat-napping on the sofa and, if a lamb was thoroughly chilled, even bringing it into the kitchen to recover before the fire. Or fed milk in which a hot poker had been plunged to raise the temperature. It was not unknown for a lamb to recline for a minute or two in the oven, the door of which was left open.

It was surprising how well a lamb survived in grim conditions when it had been licked clean and provided with milk by its mother. Orphan lambs were "a handful". A lamb that had been orphaned or had a mother short of milk was sometimes "fed a cow pap" rather than taking milk from a bottle "wi' a tit on". Pet lambs could be a nuisance. On one of the farms, a pet lamb frolicked about the farm buildings. When dipping was taking place, someone playfully dropped a pet into the noxious liquid, whereupon it ran into the house – and shook itself before the fire!

THRIFTY SHORTHORNS

Hannah had a special relationship with her cows, to the extent of giving each of them a name. In the roll of honour are Rosa (a favourite), Bumpkin, Puddles, Pushkin, Patch, Piggety, the Black Man and Her Ladyship (Rosa's daughter). Hannah fussed over them rather than just regarding them as a commercial project. In the dale-country in general, the Shorthorn was a favourite breed. It was thrifty, making few demands on the farm's resources. It was dual purpose, good for milk or beef.

When the BBC decided to film for television the best-selling vet books of James Herriot, it was planned that many of the sequences would be shot in the dale-country. Researchers were sent ahead of cast and crew to arrange for locations and properties. They must locate some cattle of the old Dales type, the period of the books being the 1930s. The researcher knew that in the 1950s a fashion began for de-horning milk cattle to reduce the risk of injury when many were kept together under new systems of management.

It was with considerable relief that the researcher visited West Park, in Baldersdale, not far from Cotherstone, where Hannah would eventually find a retirement cottage. The BBC researcher secured the co-operation of Thomas Birkett, the farmer. In a countryside now speckled by the blocky pied forms of Friesian stock, originally from the Low Countries, the gentle Shorthorn impressed by its

Hannah fussed over her cows rather than regarding them as just a commercial product. This wonderful image of milking 'Her Ladyship' captures a now bygone age.

fitness for purpose. Mr Birkett not only remained faithful to the Dairy Shorthorn, the old breed; he maintained a herd a hundred strong.

So when the Herriot films were screened, animals from Baldersdale that had been transported by road wagon to open common near the Punch Bowl Inn, Swaledale, were among the stars. In late summer, I toured the large, well-drained fields of West Park Farm, looking at old-style Shorthorns. Milk cows occupied one field. I admired the upsweeping horns, turning gracefully in at the top. If a cow had down-curving horns, it was reckoned in the dale-country that the beast was of a beefy type.

The next field held three dried-off cows and beyond was a field of bullocks.

I walked up the gently rising land to the edge of the moor. In the last good field before rough vegetation became dominant were the in-calf heifers and stirks. Young stock occupied a large pasture near the farm. There was thus a pleasing dispersal of the stock. I was shown the buildings that held the latest crop of calves – also a majestic Shorthorn bull.

The byre was fitted with a pipeline milker. Shorthorns had taken well to this relatively quiet system. Earlier units had emitted loud noises that were inclined to make the animals flighty. The Dales Shorthorn is generally very placid. As I walked among the milkers, they continued to lie down. Only two of the group eventually raised their 10 cwt forms, standing up to stretch and to stare at me. I heard that Barnard Castle had long been the marketing centre and that Thomas Birkett, like other farmers, walked surplus stock to Barnard Castle, where they were sold.

Hannah's mother had made good use of any surplus milk. The cream was skimmed off and made into butter. "In later years we got a separator, but we never got round to using it. So we put the milk into dishes and stood it on stone shelves. We then skimmed the cream off with a forefinger and put the cream in a pot to await churning day." Once a week, in summer, when there was plenty of good rich milk, it was churned. "I called it 'the happy hour', though sometimes it wasn't so happy. In thundery weather, the cream didn't churn so well. I had to turn the handle of the churn for ages. We said the cream had 'gone to sleep' and we had to give it a jolt by putting in some warm water."

The old folk remembered using the end-over-end churn, which could be hard work, especially to any child who was asked to turn the handle. If it was cool weather, you put the cream near the fire to ripen. If the cream was at a good average temperature, you might churn for about twenty minutes, otherwise it could take an hour and a-half. To ease the task and to create the right speed, a hymn was sung, the favourite being 'Onward Christian Soldiers'.

In summer, the churner might be operating for two hours before a slapping sound on the side of the churn, or a jerking of the hands, indicated that curdling had taken place. "When you got tired of churning, you peeped at the little glass window at one side to see if it was clearing. When it cleared, it was butter." Scotch Hands were used to make up the pats of butter for sale. The butter was sold at the market cross in Barnard Castle.

At West Park, Mr Birkett's mother had a high reputation for her cheese-making. The Cotherstone variety vied with that of Wensleydale in the days when cattle grazed unploughed herby ground. In the later years, the herd was milk-recorded. The yield varies, of course, but one beast yielded 1,000 gallons each lactation. Showcards tacked to the woodwork in one of the outbuildings testified to Mr Birkett's successes at the local agricultural shows, including Egglestone and Baldersdale.

The farm sustained a small flock of Teeswater sheep and some Jacob's sheep. During the 1939-45 war, horses were employed in the ploughing out of over 40 acres of ground. The fell sheep, which were Swaledales, of course, grazed the stinted acres of Cotherstone Moor. A *stint* was the pasturage of a single sheep; a specified number of stints were allocated to each cow or horse. Mutual problems regarding stints were ironed out when the stint-holders met at the *Fox* in the village each February.

IN THE HAYFIELD

Late summer. The sweet, almost sickly smell of new-mown hay fills the air. One of the most aromatic of grass species is that known as Yorkshire fog. Hannah's haytiming days were much restricted and she had – reluctantly but appreciatively, one felt – acknowledged that mechanical h.p had taken the place of true horse-power, which was in vogue for doing the heavy work on the land.

One summer's day, Freda and I arrived as a tractor-drawn baling machine, owned by friends, was disgorging neat bales of hay. Hannah, doing what jobs she could manage was keeping the sun off her head with a straw hat that had belonged to a great aunt. Hannah held a rake and watched with pleasure as a neighbour, with a tractor-drawn baler, brought the benefits of modern farming to this ancient farm. It was a time for refreshment – or *drinkings*, as the dalesfolk know it – and a lile lass settled on bales of hay and crunched her way through a packet of potato crisps.

In girlhood, Hannah had followed the mowing machine, "backing grass off" or tidying up the swathes left by the cutter bar of a single horse mowing machine. At the age of seventeen, she was forking hay into a high forking hole. There were frustrating seasons when the hay was piked [set up in heaps, to cheat a rainstorm]. As the weather improved, the pikes had to be broken into and broadcast to ensure they were dry enough to cart.

Hannah had no romantic memories of seasonal tasks like haytime. In the 1930s, when she was most involved, haytime was "tough and slogging". The

Wearing a straw hat that belonged to a great aunt, Hannah holds a rake and watches haytime operations with a cheerful smile.

*A neighbour with a tractor-drawn baler brings
the benefits of modern farming to Low Birk Hatt.*

Hauxwells were always understaffed. "Sometimes we got through haytime and
sometimes we didn't. One bad year, we 'packed in' on November 17. Then we
hadn't got it all." Horses might do the heavy work of drawing carts; otherwise
haytime was a gruelling hands-on operation. On a big farm, two horses might be
yolked to a *sweep* which collected a large quantity of hay and delivered it to the
area where it might be transferred under cover.

Each farmer was his own weather-forecaster. In chancy weather, he fretted.
When the sun shone like a blow-torch he might be heard whistling, yet if the sun
gleamed – too much, too early – it was *glisky*, unreliable. In thundery weather,
haytime was a game of chance. A method of transporting hay from awkward areas
was the horse-drawn sled, that ran smoothly over the mown or sheep-cropped
herbage.

Just before haytime, farmers in the dale had their last round of rapping their
barometers with the gusto of woodpeckers on a tree branch. Natural signs were
also used. Thomas Todd, in his *Autobiography*, relates the amusing story of a local

character who was entertaining the preacher planned for the chapel at a time when the weather was awkward. The preacher said to a guest "Who hes the weather in hand? The Almighty must be responsible; He sends everything." A farmer, looking at his flock, remarked: "He's gitten Hissel badly liked."

Once, old men donned their *keitels* [cotton jackets] and Panama hats and recalled arduous days making hay in fitful summer sunshine. They had risen at 3 a.m so as to be ready to mow at first light. Horses pulling the mowing machines must not be worked during the heat of the day. Haytime fare on the hill farms included sandwiches, cake and big pasties. Hannah had heard when the mowing was done with the aid of a scythe of awesome appearance and potential. It was straight-shafted, with a blade almost as long as a man was tall. Four men, working as a team, mowed an acre in the best part of two hours.

Attached to the shaft was a *strickle*, a four-sided length of wood pitted with many holes. With it in place, the scythe was balanced. Smeared with bacon fat, the *strickle* was dusted with fine sand to provide an abrasive surface when it was necessary to sharpen the blade. Fork and rake were the principal tools when rowing up hay to transport it into the barn. Here, the mewstead – commonly known as a moo – was oven-hot to those luckless folk who worked on it, ensuring an even spread of hay and leaving a hole in the middle to enable it to "sweat". Hay that had been taken "a bit short of dry" might fire. The old-time farmers were fussy about leaving a field clean; they did not want to see even so much as a wisp of hay on the land.

With spare time in summer, Hannah would attend to any gaps in the walls, which were "drystone", made without a dab of mortar. With a drystone wall, you got bield [shelter] for the stock. When the weather was howling cold, sheep might lie on the lee side of a wall. A drystone wall is really two walls in one, bound together with long stones known as *throughs*, packed with small stones and finished off with a row of capstones. The freeze-thaw conditions in a bad winter played havoc with weak stretches of a wall which, having been held firmly by the freeze, shifted with the thaw, hence Hannah's spell of walling.

QUESTIONS
AND ANSWERS

Now and again, I was asked to sit beside Hannah on a platform and preside over a question and answer session. This method satisfied Hannah, who did not like formal speech-making. Members of the audience had their curiosity satisfied in fine detail. Needless to say, there was a packed and attentive audience. (Hannah, the loner, became accustomed to being in a crowd. When she went to Appleby Fair, a June event attracting vast numbers of travellers with their horses, an autograph queue developed).

Sitting before a crowd of people did not faze Hannah. She was never short of an answer; indeed, the answer came within moments of the question being made. There she sat, as relaxed as if she had been at home. She wore tidy clothes, with woollen jumper and cardigan – there were no ragged ends here. She leaned forward a little and tilted her head slightly when concentrating on a question. Hannah sat upright, Dales-way, to provide the answer.

This visitor from Baldersdale was brought up in straightened times. She did not get special pleasure when recalling the old days. Each farm task had represented hard physical toil. We heard of a time when the heavy work on the farm was done by two horses – Dick and Snip. They were the pride of Hannah's

Hannah is not fazed by either crowds or special occasions.
One such event was her 60th birthday celebration in
Mickleton on August 1st, 1986.

father until he became gravely ill with pernicious anaemia and could not go outdoors. Would his faithful horses forget him? As soon as he was allowed to leave the house, he shouted for them. The horses pricked up their ears. They had not forgotten their old master.

Here, unedited, are details of a typical question and answer session, over which I presided. The gathering, at Cross Hills, an Airedale village, was preceded, Yorkshirewise, by Frank Smith's choir singing the hymn *Sweet is the Work* to the tune Deep Harmony.

There you were, left alone on the farm. I gather the season you did not like was winter...

I used to have a saying – in winter I exist and in summer I live. A marked distinction.
[Hannah turned to me and remarked: "You sent me a postcard from where you were on holiday, emphasising the blue sky."]

In winter, it would be just incessant work with the cattle.

Yes. I'm still not improving with age. I've always been slow. And I'm still slow. And there wasn't any modern aids. Everything was to traipse about with.

How many cows had you got?

When I left there were seven. It wasn't a lot, I know. Once I was working away in the byre on a winter's day. The job in hand was taking me long enough. I saw a neighbour across at Close Lodge come down to his field house where he maybe had more cattle than I had everywhere. And he was done, and all them done, and back up home – and I was still pottering on with my few.

You had some grim experiences in winter.

One of the grimmest was when the electricity went off. Electricity was the only thing I had. The fireplace wasn't any good. The chimney was blocked. When the electricity went off, there was no heating, no hot water, no nothing. As I was carrying water and digging out, the big Army coat I wore got wet, then frozen. You don't appreciate things when they're functioning.

What are the little pleasures you enjoy most about your present home at Cotherstone?

The heating. And the bathroom. I was just thinking yesterday – when I was late, as always when getting ready – I haven't the kettle to boil and a pan of water to boil up. And I hadn't a bucket of cold water to mix in when it got hot. I also like having things handy – the shop, for instance – instead of having to traipse all over for everything. Those are some of the things. And I'm handy to the chapel when I'm able to go, which is not as much as I would like.

Do you ever feel like going back to the farm?

It's my home no longer. If I got homesick and wanted to go back it would be domino. I miss the animals. I miss the trees, the space and the water. Sometimes I miss the walkers on the Pennine Way.

What did you think about at the farm when spring was on the way?

I did like the return of the tewits [lapwings]. Sometimes there was bad weather after they came but they told me that spring would be coming before long.

Has appearing on television changed your life dramatically?

I've got my old clothes still. And I've got a little dog, Tim.

Is Tim good?

Well – he's a Jack Russell and Jack Russells can vary. He's a nice nature but he doesn't like other dogs, especially his own kind. I generally take him out for a walk into the field behind the garage because there's less chance of meeting other people with their dogs. That field is my saving grace. It's quiet.

What do you think of London? You've spent a fair bit of time there in recent years.

I like to go to London – but wouldn't want to live there. It is our capital. I like to see buildings I've read about. And to see names on streets.

You've been abroad? You didn't seem to like the high hills.

No – I'd had enough of them. The hills are not like our hills. They are grey and forbidding.

Can the shop at Cotherstone meet all your requirements?

Yes – it's a grand shop. There's brushes and buckets, clothes pegs, clothes lines, electrical goods, even aspirins and sewing thread. You name it. The shopkeeper has it.

This is the end of the first half. The Americans call it an intermission. We are going to sample tea and biscuits. Afterwards, would you mind if people asked questions?

Oh, no – that's all right. I'll do my best to answer. If there's an embarrassing one or something I don't want to answer, then I reserve that right.

What is your present routine at home?

Tim has to have his walk. Then I've got to have my breakfast. Then, I maybe go to the shop. One of the things in the village, which is a mixed blessing, is that you'll meet someone in the shop or coming in or going out. When I'm taking the dog, it's the same thing. Chatting with people is a lovely feature of village life. Except, of course, when you're in a hurry.

What happened when you left the farm to attend a garden party at Buckingham Palace?

I think somebody came to the iron gate for me. And then went to Darlington station. It was July and it was cold and wet. Fortunately it did fair-out. At the palace, I was just one among thousands. It was a thrill to walk through the gate. And the policemen were nice. And, of course, it was a thrill to see the Sovereign. And to hear the National Anthem played in the Sovereign's presence.

At other times, the Queen might be wearing wellies.

Not being presumptuous, we do share one or two things. (Laughter). She often wears a headscarf, which I like too. I'm wearing a Scottish scarf at the moment. It belonged to a relative – and it's mended, by the way.

It's called re-cycling in the Dales.

I've had a bit of practice at that.

[There followed questions from members of the audience.]

Are you a good weather forecaster?

No. Not really. Years ago when the fire was going and smoke puffed down, it was going to come wild and wet. In haytime, if the seagulls were coming up, we thought the weather was going to change. And, of course, if the wind gets into the north and the east, in the winter months, you get bad weather. Except in summertime, we used to get good hay weather from the east. But I've no idea what the weather's going to be.

Do you still play the piano?

Mainly the organ [harmonium] but the bellows are damaged. I can't get any sound. I'm going to get it mended or get something to play on. I have no ability but if I'm away at a concert or something, and hear something I like, it would be nice to play the tune when I got home. I like "Deep Harmony".

I understand you don't watch the clock, Hannah.

My clock can be two hours fast. (Laughter). And still I'm late (More laughter). One clock loses and I keep pushing it on a bit when I wind it up. I usually take it to bed with me. And I push the clock on half an hour. Then when I get up I find it is half an hour later that I thought it was.

Hannah, you've had a rough life. If you had your time to do over again, would you do anything different?

I suppose in the same circumstances, I'd have done the same again.

What did you dream about doing when you were young?

I wish I'd been a good organist. Like Reginald Fort. Or somebody like that.

On your travels, what did you think of Venice and the Orient Express?

It was one of the highlights of the trip. Pictures or film don't prepare you for what I term an "inland sea". It was lovely. I'd go back – in fact, I said when we reached Boulogne to come home, I wouldn't mind going back again. It fell on deaf ears. No one seemed to take any notice. And the Orient Express, it was a wonderful experience.

Was there a murder on the Orient Express?

Not when I was there. But you can imagine it happening. It's an ideal situation.

What's it like being a celebrity?

I don't think of myself as a celebrity; I'm just me. And hope to remain so. Just a plain daleswoman. Up the dale, one was somewhat limited for companionship, for talk. The folk living nearest to me talked mainly about the weather in winter-time and when it was lambing time; it was the same at haytime. Then when it got to back-end, and there was talk about what the trade was like. Talk was limited. That's why I enjoyed chatting with walkers on the Pennine Way.

What was it like being alone on winter nights?

Well, I was occupied in wintertime. It took me a long time to do my jobs. I'd to get hay to the cattle up the fields. There was a lot of carrying. And cleaning byres out. After I got the electricity put in, I listened to the radio or watched television or read a bit. I did go twice – once for three weeks and another time for nearly three weeks – without seeing anybody. But time didn't hang on my hands.

Hannah, do you ever throw anything away?

No.

Is Cotherstone the Promised Land after your spell in the wilderness?

It's a nice place to live. I was lucky. There were people living there I knew; they had lived up the dale. There's always something going on.

Do they still make cheese out of blue milk and have to attack it with an axe?

It's made somewhere. And they sell it at the post office. I'm not a cheese lover. The only time I eat that sort of cheese is with a fruit cake or something. The present 'Cutherstun' cheese is a crumbly cheese. Rather a light cheese.

[Frank Smith and his choir rounded off the afternoon by rendering their version of 'Sing a Song of Sixpence'.]

HANNAH'S CHRISTMAS

The festival season, a bright period in the drab winter, was to Hannah just another spell of work with her livestock. I asked Hannah about the previous Christmas. She could not recall a single visitor, though someone had been to see her on Boxing Day. A pause, then: "I wish it was always summer". During the week before Christmas in 1978, she tied up the cattle in the byres and resigned herself to the extra work this would involve. No one called that Christmas Day. Meanwhile, groups of walkers on the Pennine Way bade her good day. When the electrical power failed, her trusty Army greatcoat – of 1939 vintage – insulated her from the sub-zero temperatures outside.

Within the house, she swaddled herself in clothes as well as blankets. One of the items of clothing she spread over herself was a tweed coat that had belonged to an uncle. There was an electrical failure. On each of the days she was without power, her only form of lighting was a stable lamp. Hannah had but one meal a day, this consisting of a cold drink and some corned beef, with a cold drink before bed at night. It was not that she was without food. The effort of coping with the cattle in grim weather left her little energy to care for herself. A coal fire was out of the question. The chimneys were blocked.

It was a memorable time when she became aware that the power had been restored by the valiant men of the electricity authority. The preparation of a mug of tea was delayed because a layer of ice had formed in the electric kettle. She had

Overwhelmed by an avalanche of mail at Christmas 1974.

Winter in Lunedale, the tributary valley immediately to the north of Baldersdale,

first to warm water in a pan to thaw out the ice. When a blizzard re-arranged the contours of the fields, and they were crusted with ice, Hannah hauled bales of hay across the glassy surface of the fields on a home-made sled.

She considered that she might survive, in a fashion, on a stock of potatoes and "tins and things" but she has a fondness for butter and cheese. Her routine did not permit her much time for cooking. In the autumn of 1978, she recalled two notable items of self-help. She had baked a local dish called tharf and two apple pies.

A few old men believed the cattle in the byre knelt down on Christmas morning in honour of the Christ Child. The children awoke to find stockings holding a few nuts, an orange and perhaps a sugar mouse, its tail made of wool. There was usually goose for dinner – with enough grease produced in the cooking to preserve in jars against the time when children risking chesty complaints had those chests anointed with grease. Goose wings were bundled up to be used at spring-cleaning time. There was nothing like a wing for removing cobwebs from behind large items of furniture.

To a farmer in the upper dales, mid-winter did not occur at Christmas but in February, when townsfolk are looking out for the first signs of spring and the dale-country farmer anxiously scanned his barn, hoping to have at least half his stock of hay. In the February of 1984, journalist June Hawdon, of the *Evening Despatch*, popped in to see Hannah. Unopened parcels, many from Christmas, and the Christmas cards, were stacked against a wall. Said Hannah: "I've never had time to open them."

How had she fared during her eighteen years of self-dependence since her lonely life in Baldersdale had been revealed to the nation? And, especially, how was she coping with another long winter? It had not been too severe, even though she had been up and about early, digging a way through snow. "I had my breakfast and went to bed...I was exhausted," said Hannah. Admitted to the house, the journalist found that what, many years before, had been a roaring coal fire had been replaced by a "pitiful little two-bar electric fire". The visitor looked into a dark and dingy room, in which cobwebs were hanging from the ceiling. There remained the mound of unopened parcels. Hannah had no spare time to attend to them.

The only source of water was still the trickle across the field – "there's none on tap". For Hannah, now aged 57, winter days were not long enough. "She toils away, bringing more pails of water, lumping more hay into the byre – all the time talking to her Bumpkin and her Rosa." Inquisitive folk and well-wishers were among dozens of visitors who turned up at Low Birk Hatt. Years after television

Deep midwinter was the time when Hannah could become weary of the demands made on her by her cattle. Taking bales of hay out into the fields was back-breaking work.

introduced Hannah to the people, some still wrote to her and sent her parcels. Hannah's lifestyle, "apart from a handful of Cinderella-type visits to the outside world", had changed little. She was glad of so many blessings. She might watch television – when she had the time. If time permitted, she might cook herself a meal on a modern electric cooker sent by one of her fans.

Hannah both loved and hated her cattle. She most certainly liked them, but was sometimes weary of the demands they made on her time and energy. In general, as the milk demand increased, the still popular Shorthorn got a "smittlin" of other breeds, notably the Ayrshire, to boost production. In chats I had with farmers I heard that if a man was not particular about the type of bull he used, the quality of the old stock would decline.

Buying a bull in the days before the introduction of artificial insemination was a chancy operation unless the farmer went to a dealer with a good name. Few farmers trusted a bull and with good cause. Each year one or two dale-farmers were injured or gored when what had seemed to be a docile animal turned on them. August was a particularly unreliable month. It was then that a bull made a terrible noise and sent sods flying.

As Hannah endured her fiftieth winter at Low Birk Hatt, gales pounded her house, loosening yet more slates, and snowdrifts arched themselves against the buildings. Hannah closed her eyes, leaned back in a chair and dreamt about what she imagined the Mediterranean to be like – blue sky, blue sea. The winter of 1978 left the inevitable legacy of work. Some of the drystone walls that were gapped remained gapped. A number of slates on the outbuildings were still deranged. Winter overlapped spring. The summer seemed pitifully brief, with the days apparently rushing by towards yet another winter. "Only the weeds seem to thrive," said Hannah. "It's amazing how they recover after a bad winter."

Turning out day for stock occurs in late April, even early May. One couple released their stock from the byre and it snowed during the night. Early next day, the farmer looked out over the white landscape. He roused his sleeping wife with the words: "Nay, Betty – we've slept aw summer." Hannah was not ruled by the clock and sometimes a cow or two would do its best to avoid capture at milking time. Milk drawn from the cows was not retailed, being available for the young stock, for her pets and, in modest quantities, for herself, though Hannah was not keen on drinking milk.

SIGNED WITH A FLOURISH

There were book signings galore. Hannah took the work seriously. A few wriggly lines might suffice for many another celebrity. Hannah was painstaking. She signed "Hannah B.T – for Bayles Tallentire – Hauxwell". She didn't like to think that an old family name would pass out of use. Hannah delighted those who bought books by the time and care she put into her signing. Apart from her signature, she included the name of the recipient and the date, which plainly did not fit in with modern business practices, which involved shifting books quickly.

Title page of the author's copy of Hannah's North Country, *signed in typical style. It is not surprising that lengthy queues developed at bookshops.*

HANNAH'S NORTH COUNTRY

HANNAH HAUXWELL
with BARRY COCKCROFT

To Freda & Bill.
With Best Wishes.
Hannah Hauxwell.
December 3rd 1993.

CENTURY
London Sydney Auckland Johannesburg

Above: The long wait! Customers queue patiently at Dressers in Darlington to get their fully inscribed copy of Seasons of My Life.

Opposite: Hannah takes a break from signing during a visit to Leeds in the 1980s.

Freda and I have a book which takes in our names, her full name and the date. Inevitably, a queue developed. At the Craven Herald shop in Skipton, Hannah was still signing books when closing time arrived. A line of people stretched through the premises and part way down the High Street. Their patience was rewarded with signed books – and cups of coffee! At Posthorn Books at Settle, when the signing was accomplished, Hannah light-heartedly offered to sign books other than her own. The circumstances of a book-signing at Dressers in Darlington, on an October day in the 1970s, formed the subject of a long article in the local newspaper. A photograph showed a section of the crowd, with Hannah in the middle giving the royal type of wave to the photographer. "I touched her, I touched her," cried a middle-aged woman, adding: "She was just a foot away and I touched her." In short, Hannah briefly stopped the traffic.

The general manager of the store – and Hannah's chauffeur for the day – had never expected, or seen, anything like it. The crowd, hundreds strong, clapped and cheered. Hannah, 47, and wearing her best frock for the occasion, responded cheerfully. In the boss's office, she acknowledged that it was all "very nice" and she was enjoying the event, "but it'll still be nice to get back. There's a lot of work to do." Three heavy staff members cleared the way for her entry into the book department, where she was to autograph copies of *Hannah in Yorkshire*, published by the *Dalesman* in association with Yorkshire Television.

Jolly Jack (J B Priestley) had commented: "Everyone who loves the Yorkshire Dales should acquire and cherish this book." Dressers had purchased 200 copies – and they sold the lot. Those who handed over their books for signature included a sprinkling of people who had connections with Hannah, such as the lady who remarked: "You know my brother; he used to sit beside you at Chapel" and a more athletic type who said: "We've met before. I walked past your farm." Hannah, frail-looking but head above water, asked each person what inscription they would like. And by the time the last of the multitude had gone to their homes, everyone was happy. And, as the newspaper report concluded, "Hannah was going back to her splendid isolation."

CHAPEL DAYS

On Sunday, in Hannah's young days, a deafening hush descended on the dale country. Six days shalt thou labour; Sunday is for vital jobs, such as caring for the farm stock, but mainly for worship, for meditation. Ideally it was a quiet day, so quiet you might hear the wax crackling in your ears. Pious families wended their way along farm tracks and the roadway, heading for Church or Chapel. A sharp distinction was drawn between the two.

The Church operated with a parish system – almost invariably one church, one parish. Chapels, on the other hand, untrammelled by the weight of history, were less pretentious and much more numerous. Most of them rose with a burst of religious fervour in the later part of the nineteenth century. Inscribed in stone above the doorway or high up on the front wall is the date of opening in good, solid Victorian lettering.

Hannah was baptised an Anglican but, with her mother and grandma, often attended a little Methodist church, which – like many another in the dale-country – was single-storey, boxlike, with sloping roof and a porch stuck on as though it was an afterthought. The pews were hard except where a family, sitting regularly in a specific pew, overlaid the seat with pads, usually of red and black.

A Methodist chapel had a pulpit with a rostrum firm enough for the preacher to lean on when he was being conversational and so firm it might carry a heavy Bible and endure thumping as emotional local preachers emphasised important points in their sermons. Hannah enjoyed the warmth of the worship and lusty hymn-singing. She was less fond of the tedious length of many a sermon.

T'Chapil, being as austere and unpretentious as the dalesfolk themselves, usually had a sandwich type of service – hymn, prayer, hymn, lesson, etc. There was pride in the chapel. Its interior was spick and span. Flowers on the

With her mother and grandma, Hannah often attended a small Methodist chapel that was like many another in the dale-country. This particular example is at Garsdale; the Settle to Carlisle railway is in the background.

communion table were provided by ladies whose names (and the dates when their floral gifts should be made) were prominently dispayed near the entrance.

In the smallest, a harmonium provided the musical accompaniment. A story told of one remote chapel concerned the harmonium, which was being played by an old lady to whom the instrument still had mysteries. She did her best. The wailing sound irritated the preacher, who leaned towards her and said: "Aye, lass, can't we have a more up to date tune?" She is said to have replied: "You can't have it more modern than this – I'm making it up as I go on!"

Praise and prayer were robust when delivered by local preachers who were truly local, known to all. The classic form of a sermon was an introduction, three relevant points and a summing up. People began to relax when point three was announced. Anglicans were less intense in their sermonising. One of the congregation, an old chap, hearing an argument about religion, retorted: "If t'prayer books reight – its reight. If not, clap it at t'back o' t'fire."

Hannah was fond of recalling that the great days in the Methodist year were

Methodist choir in the spick and span interior of Garsdale chapel.

the Sunday School and Chapel Anniversaries. "We had relatives living at
Newhouses, not far from the school. I was asked for tea just before the Sunday
School Anniversary. They had a lovely house and served lovely meals. Then we
went up to Chapel in the evening to practise singing for the Anniversary. On the
day itself, the place was packed. Then we'd go down to Newhouses again for our
tea." Celebrations extended from Saturday to Monday night, with suppers at the
Chapel on the first and last evenings."

In 1990, in a series of Sunday evening television programmes called *Highway*,
Sir Harry Secombe called on Hannah at Cotherstone. He had previously been in
Teesdale, where people talked and sang about the dale. At Newbiggin, a supporter
of the Methodist chapel told Harry that John Wesley had visited the place eleven
times and had preached from the pulpit fitted in the chapel. Harry asked her why
Methodism had made such an appeal to the dalesfolk. She said: "It gave poor
people a sense of worth and dignity. It broadened their horizons." Hannah was
filmed as he sat in her living room. Asked about her retirement, she said that she

A harmonium – music-maker in many chapels.

enjoyed it very nicely, thank you.

As she grew up in Baldersdale, her little library was dominated by books of a religious nature. She was aware of the strong influence exerted by the Methodist chapel. Her family not only devoutly attended worship whenever it was held, they had a religious library at home. Through attendance at the Sunday School, she was able to join the coach trips that were organised to seaside resorts and the Lake District.

The chapel attended by Hannah is closed. So is the school, which is now a youth centre. Methodism in the remaining chapels, of various denominations, is less robust than early last century, when older men would thump the pews in their excitement and Sunday School teachers – farm labourers among them – thought nothing of landing the Bible at a scholar who was causing offence.

When I next meet Hannah I must tell her about my father, a local preacher, visiting a little dale-country chapel to preach. He was greeted by the chapel-keeper, who lived in rooms on the ground floor. She led the way up steep steps to the chapel, which occupied the upper part of the building. A Rhode Island Red hen ran up before them. It apparently laid eggs in the vestry. There were three people present during that service – father, the chapel-keeper and an old man who was hard of hearing. As the chapel-keeper (who was also the organist) passed him on her way to the organ stool, she said: "Cut thee sermon short when thou smells t'Yorkshire pudding."

FLITTING TO COTHERSTONE

When the farm sale was imminent, Hannah – aged 62 - began to think about what a journalist called "the daunting reality of moving". Yet it was nobbut six miles to Cotherstone. Sealed tenders for the farm were opened, but Hannah asked for a fortnight to consider them before moving to her new home. There was a deadline for quitting the farm – December 18. "I've never sold a farm before," she said smiling. "It's a very big thing to have to do. Once in a lifetime is enough. I just like jogging gently along. I don't enjoy the business side of things at all. And I don't like having to make decisions. I'm just starting squaring up in the house and neighbours are lending me boxes."

There were attractions in flitting – as they say in the Dales. The Cotherstone cottage was warm and complete with hot and cold running water. "When the leaves start to fall out here, it strikes a chill to the heart. It's rather nice to think I won't have another long winter up here. As you get older, I think you fall out of love with winter." Press reports on the flit to Cotherstone referred to "Hermit Hannah" and "the twinkle-eyed spinster". A photograph showing Hannah with a paraffin lamp and an unshielded electric bulb (lit) was captioned "Light Years Away".

Hannah told reporter Cliff Edwards: "The winters are getting too much for me. It's difficult breaking the ice on the stream to get at the drinking water for me and the cattle. I get so tired after mucking out or throwing the hay down in the snow. I'll have to wait and see if I can cope with the noise in the village and the sound of the cars. But it will be nice to have so many people about. " She would miss

Low Birk Hatt on December 14th 1988 – four days before the deadline for quitting the farm.

A ferocious-looking iron mangle is among the paraphernalia assembled outside the farmhouse on the same day.

Sadly and alone, Hannah ponders on her Low Birk Hatt years as removal men take her possessions down to a new home at Cotherstone.

standing in the doorway of the byre after working all day and, as already mentioned, the silver and gold effects from a full moon on rippling water.

Yorkshire Television filmed her in the initial stage of finding a suitable cottage. An auctioneer took her from cottage to cottage. His task was to find accommodation that suited a maiden lady with a dog and a load of souvenirs from the past. Into view, in due course, came the cottage she still occupies – a cottage that Freda and I visited, on the first occasion being greeted by Hannah with the words: "Come in – I still haven't unpacked."

We felt very much at home amid the unpacked boxes and heaps of smaller possessions. The contrast with the first entry of Hannah, caught on film as she was shown round by the previous owner, was startling. Then, everything had been colourful, neat. She was shown into an immaculate bathroom and rejoiced that ere long she would soon have the benefit of bathing in warm water, freshly drawn from a shining tap.

Two decades after *Too Long a Winter*, the team was back to record Hannah's last days at Low Birk Hatt. Two men – an auctioneer and John Geldard, a long-time farmer friend of Hannah – toured the fields and the buildings to assess their worth so there would be realistic prices at the sale. The land seemed in good heart but might benefit here and there from drainage. One of the men found a particularly wet spot. It was deep enough for water to slop into his wellies.

Interior shots in this follow-up film reveal that Hannah had little surplus energy for household tasks. She appears never to have thrown anything away, not even used food tins. When Freda and I visited Low Birk Hatt, we saw only the kitchen and a living room in which there was little spare room in which to move and where a chair was covered by the ubiquitous plastic fertiliser sack.

Now, in film, we were taken into a large bedroom containing Hannah's four-poster bed and little else. We had seen (on film, in an unaccustomed blaze of electric arc lamps) Hannah carefully peeling back bedclothes and clambering wearily into bed, clad in a thick nightdress and, as a last duty, reaching out to switch off the normal low-power electric light.

Filming reached fever pitch on sale day. There was a goodly crowd. The auctioneer, with his stick, went through the timeless routine of giving everyone a chance to buy a succession of lots, including a careworn settee, which cleared the £100 mark. The cattle were taken over by a neighbouring farmer; there was a sad parting between Hannah and her bovine friends in the long lane leading up to the farm buildings.

As the cattle were being coaxed down the lane, one of them butted a fence,

HANNAH'S MEADOW
Purchase assisted by
THE FOUR WINDS TRUST
in memory of
RUTH GILLETT
who loved flowers

breaking a length of wood. Hannah carefully replaced it. The Good Neighbour who was taking over the cattle appeared from a bank of mist. He assured Hannah that her cattle would be well cared for. They departed, leaving Hannah to ponder, sadly and alone, on her Low Birk Hatt years.

The film ended with the packing in a furniture van of the household items that would find a place at a new home. There was, of course, a long-case clock and Grannie's photograph in its big wooden frame. The landscape was obligingly snowbound. Hannah must not be filmed leaving in sunshine! A tractor was summoned to tow the furniture van on a potentially slippery track. Against a setting sun, of course.

In October, 1988, as Hannah was keenly anticipating her move to the warmth of a cottage in Cotherstone, it was announced that Low Birk Hatt, Hannah's old farmhouse, and 15 acres, had been sold to an anonymous bidder from Cleveland. A further 42 acres went to a local farmer and the remaining 28 acres of meadow and pastureland were bought by the Durham Wildlife Trust, which planned to set up a nature reserve at what was regarded as one of the best remaining examples of a hay meadow in this part of the Pennines.

Members of Durham Wildlife Trust walk through Hannah's Meadow after the official unveiling of a plaque in June 1990.

ABBOT HALL

The manager of Abbot Hall, at Kents Bank, on the northern shore of Morecambe Bay, was keen to have Hannah as one of the speakers when a large group of local people met at the guest house to listen to a worthwhile address and have light refreshments. I was a regular visitor to the Hall, where I took courses with a Lake District theme. Having mentioned Hannah in one of my talks, I was asked for details of where she lived. The upshot was the first of a goodly number of visits. Hannah became so familiar with Abbot Hall, a plaque was affixed to the bedroom she occupied and on the noticeboard was a message from her: "North, South, East and West – Abbot Hall is still the best."

As mentioned, Hannah did not like to give a straight talk; she responded best to questions. Therefore, for the umpteenth time, I was asked to pose questions and

Abbot Hall at Kents Bank where Hannah became a regular visitor.

Opposite: Hannah has an unusual companion during one of her visits to Abbot Hall!

then invited queries from the audience. The result was that hearers had a special insight into the life of a remarkable woman. She was not accustomed to community activity, but took part in some of the evening socials, especially carpet bowls, though the bowls she sent along the carpet laid down the centre of the hall invariably went off course and collided with the piano legs.

The most memorable gathering took place in tiny Cartmel Methodist Church, into which were crammed Hannah, me, the Abbot Hall manager, the Cockfield Methodist Male Voice Choir – and a congregation of nearly a hundred. Once again, I sat beside her, asking questions, before inviting the congregation to join in. The Cockfield Methodist Male Voice Choir provided musical intermissions. Hannah beamed when they sang, for this was her favourite choir, emanating from the northern dales. Cockfield is a former mining village situated between Barnard Castle and Bishop Auckland.

Hannah first heard the choir during her schooldays. They were singing in harmony at the anniversary services in Baldersdale chapel. Their leader, George Tallentire Dickinson, was related to Hannah on the Tallentire side. In wartime, the choir had formed a concert party; songs were interspersed with monologues. Edwin Coates, on leave from service in the RAF, became one of the keenest supporters. Subsequently, he became leader of the choir. Edwin provided accordion accompaniment as required.

Years later, when Hannah was ensconced at Low Birk Hatt, members of the choir, led by Edwin, responded to a viewing of the film *Too Long a Winter* by travelling to Baldersdale in cars, then trudging through the fields to arrive at the back door of Low Birk Hatt for a surprising, and astonishing, reunion with Hannah. Her harmonium was played. Favourite hymns were sung. Edwin returned later with his accordion and serenaded a delighted Hannah.

When she appeared in the national television series, *This is Your Life*, it was the Cockfield Choir who brought the programme harmoniously to a close. At the Cartmel event, a tape recording of choral singing, entitled Hannah Hauxwell's Favourites, was available for purchase. Here was gospel singing, rendered with warmth and gusto. Incidentally, the seating capacity of Cartmel chapel on that memorable evening when both Hannah and choir performed was so fully occupied that the chairman had to sit on the floor.

LAKE DISTRICT INTERLUDE

Freda and I were to give Hannah a sortie into the Lake District. In 1989, when Hannah, aged 62 years, reluctantly swapped her farmhouse for a cottage in the village of Cotherstone, four miles away, she was spending a few days at Abbot Hall during one of my Lakeland courses. I usually arranged for a mid-week break – an afternoon off, during which those on the course might stroll into Grange to do some shopping.

Hannah was viewing her move to relative civilisation with mixed feelings. She had told one of his visitors: "I will miss most the moonlight when it touches the water across the dale, with the dark hills behind. Oh, that is magnificent. I do hear that many young people today have no knowledge of the countryside and I find that sad. One can be rich in a town. But to be in the fresh air and see the beauty of such a place as my old farm is a wondrous thing."

We who had seen her television debut in *Too Long a Winter* now shared her pleasure in being escorted to various parts of Europe and the New World courtesy of Yorkshire Television. Hannah, who had lived a parochial life, could now talk – though never boastfully – about experiences in the United States and Switzerland. On a modest scale was the excursion that my wife and I planned during a spare afternoon at Abbot Hall. We would take her to the head of Great Langdale.

But first, we stood on the wooded eastern shore of Coniston Water as the steamer built by the Furness Railway and now owned by the National Trust went regally by. Hannah's fancy had been taken not by a Victorian steamboat but by a fallen tree branch which, unlike the proverbial rolling stone, had gathered moss.

Top: Hannah likes English hills. She was impressed with Pike o' Stickle at the head of Great Langdale, which she found especially appealing.

The Victorian steamboat Gondola on Coniston Water.

Above: With their white faces and coarse wool, Herdwick sheep are an appealing breed unique to the Lakeland fells.

Left: A Lake District farmer, photographed at Wasdale Show.

She insisted on it being placed in the car (and, back at Abbot Hall, it would be given a prominent place in her bedroom). Our Lakeland adventure continued.

I drove to Skelwith Bridge where, our appetites sharpened by crisp Lakeland air, we visited the cafe. Hannah insisted on paying for our repast. We had restrained ourselves; she joyfully chose whatever was offered. A buttered scone was ordered. Did we also want jam? Hannah assuredly did. "Cream?" "Yes, please." A mile or so away, I parked the car near Skelwith Falls. We stood on bare rock and watched the river go white with fury as it was pent in and we had a feeling that the rocks might be shivering under our feet.

Here was the best of Lakeland, revealed by sunlight, in air crisp and clean. We looked over a vast expanse of meadowland – a sort of miniature prairie where one would have expected the upper dale to be rocky and narrow. The sunlit Langdale Pikes rose like a backcloth for grand opera. Hannah was not impressed. She came from an area where horizons were low. Lofty mountains did not appeal to her. (It amused me, when a filmed record of her visit to the Alps was televised, to note Hannah's response to the scene. She was taken to a vantage point backed by lofty, snow-capped mountains. Said Hannah: "I don't like mountains").

She was interested in the Herdwick, t'auld breed, peculiar to the Lakeland fells. Small, big-boned, with faces white as hoar frost and bodies swathed in coarse wool, they scanned the world with eyes that looked half as old as time. The wool used to be woven as the celebrated "hodden grey", as worn by John Peel, the huntsman. Herdwicks might look alike but a Lakeland shepherd could see subtle differences in appearance and gait. He also had recourse to the lug [ear] mark. Since Norse times it has been customary to clip pieces from an ear to distinguish one flock from another.

I mentioned the Shepherds Meets, when farmers as well as shepherds gathered at traditional places to return any stray sheep to their rightful owners. The men then headed for a nearby hostelry to sample the Tatie Pot, a meal of grand proportions. I told Hannah that when I joined such a feast, we sat at a long table, adorned with the usual cutlery and also with huge jars of pickles, piccalilli and beetroot. The Tatie Pot was as thick as the *poddish* [porridge] mentioned in an old account – poddish so thick that a mouse might walk dryshod across it. Following the poddish were pie and custard, the whole washed down by good strong tea.

HANNAH-BY-THE-SEA

Another time when Hannah was staying as a guest at Abbot Hall and I was taking a Lakeland course, I slipped away in the evening and strode along the Bayside path to see Cedric Robinson and Olive, his wife, at the house traditionally reserved for the Guide to the Sands. As usual, I was invited in. And as usual, Olive provided me with a cup of tea. When Hannah's name bobbed up in conversation, and I revealed that she was currently staying at Abbot Hall, Cedric and Olive were rapturous. They had respected her for years and intended, one day, to make their way to her high-dale farm.

The fact that she was less than a mile away – and that Cedric was a regular visitor to Abbot Hall, talking about his life on the Bay – drove any other thought out of our minds. I fixed up a meeting between Hannah and Cedric via David. They hit it off right away, to use his own words. Hannah was due to return home on the following day, but there was time to visit Cedric and Olive at their home, which also presides over a smallholding, run on traditional lines, with the animals regarded as pets – as, indeed, was the case with Hannah and her cows in Baldersdale.

Hannah, with her typical down-to-earth approach to life, advised Cedric when there was a calving problem. She said that modern methods did not always work. And when they failed, they led to a lot of vet's bills. Hannah switched her attention to the small tract of meadowland and methods of hay-making. She even offered to

Cedric Robinson and Hannah
beside the shore of Morecambe
Bay at Kents Bank.

Top: 'Sandpiper Two', the tractor-hauled trailer that is used by Cedric to take people out onto the Sands.

Bottom left: Welcome guests at Guide's Farm, the home of Cedric and Olive Robinson. Left to right: Olive, Lavinia Thwaites, Cedric and Hannah.

Bottom right: Hannah outside Abbot Hall with Cedric's father William Robinson.

return at haytime and lend a hand.

A television company arranged to film Hannah and Cedric as she was conveyed on the Sands in a tractor-hauled, two-wheeled trailer, named Sandpiper, with seats for several people and canvas as a roof to deflect any rain. (Subsequently, a larger, firm-roofed trailer was introduced and named Sandpiper Two.) When a new edition of the book *Sand Pilot of Morecambe Bay* was published in 1998, the foreword was under the name of Hannah Hauxwell, who stayed with Cedric and Olive for a week, accompanying Cedric on signing sessions.

The two of them had a "live" attendance at Radio Blackburn, a memorable occasion on which there was a heavy snowfall that, happily, thawed enough to allow them to return safely to Kents Bank. They took time out for a walk along the foreshore at Kents Bank Farm, along with Olive and Lavinia Thwaites, Hannah's good friend from her village of Cotherstone.

SAYINGS OF HANNAH

I don't like handling money. In money matters,
I put the brake on – and keep it on.

I'll have a bath if a friend is going to call.

I hear that many young people have no knowledge
of the countryside, which is sad.

I endured too many winters.

I'm not a Christmassy person now.

MALLERSTANG OCCASION

Hannah was, for several pleasant days, a guest of the Hasteds, whose home – a former railway cottage – stands near the highpoint of the Settle-Carlisle railway. It was a novelty for Hannah to hear the rumble of trains on the railway, which hereabouts ran on a ledge cut from the flanks of Wild Boar Fell. Hannah, having been invited to a flower festival at St Mary's in Mallerstang, was driven across Stainmore on the wide road that replaced a glorified cart-track. She was seeing it for only the second time and was inclined to call it the "new road".

In Mallerstang, where the River Eden has its nursery reaches, Hannah was in something like a trough between Mallerstang Edge, soaring steeply for almost 2,000-ft, and the ponderous, flat-topped Wild Boar Fell. The dale itself had all the typical features of a glacier-hewn valley. At that time of year the meadows were lushy green; there was a familiar pattern of drystone walls, some ponies on the common – and her destination: the little church.

Hannah was taken along a slate path to where, above the porch, she might read an inscription lauding the generosity of Lady Anne Clifford, who had been something of a queen in the northern dales because of her vast estates. I suspected that Anne was a woman after Hannah's heart – methodical and capable of many

St Mary's Church in Mallerstang, decorated for the flower show which Hannah attended.

Inscribed tablet over the porch commemorating the
generosity of Lady Anne Clifford in restoring the church.

acts of kindness.

What struck Hannah most about the church were its "big thick walls, the woodwork – oak, I suppose – like silk to the touch. I enjoyed the organ. The people were friendly." The Vicar had taken a photograph of her. Hannah was told he was an enthusiastic fan of railways, especially the Settle-Carlisle line. Hearing that there was to be a special steam train on a Sunday, Hannah sympathised, adding: "They should take Vicars into consideration when they plan rail trips on Sundays."

I joined her at the flower festival. Then – early next day – I tracked her down to the home of the Hasteds. Asked what time she had got up, Hannah replied that she did not know. "The clock had stopped." What were her impressions of Mallerstang and St Mary's Church? Hannah, sitting in the "front" room of the house, wearing woollen jumper and cardigan – almost as much wool, indeed, as on a fell-going sheep – said: "The valley is lovely in its own way. Wild. Peaceful. Great big hills."

Hannah was taken into the adjacent cafe, where the only patrons were two couples who had been friendly when living at Keld in Swaledale but now – at home in the Eden Valley – enjoyed revisiting their old haunts. One of the men raised a laugh when he said, of Hannah's cattle, as featured in the film *Too Long a Winter*: "I could never understand how well those bullocks were looking when they were out in the snow." Said an amused Hannah: "I used to like to give plenty to them in summertime and winter."

Chris, a local farmer, persuaded her to ride pillion on his Quad or ATV – all-terrain vehicle – one of the three-wheeled variety. She eventually appeared from the house clad as though for a major expedition. She wore a green woolly cap and a coat that almost reached her ankles. In the period before Health and Safety became major legal requirements, Hannah, determined not to catch a chill while travelling in moorland air, perched on one of the mudguards, over a rear wheel, looking anxiously now and again in case her long coat was trailing.

Chris was away for perhaps half an hour. Using the all-terrain characteristic of his powerful little vehicle, he took Hannah on the track beside Hell Gill and almost to within patting distance of some of sheep on the skirts of the fell. Then they were back again, across the railway bridge, to her temporary lodgings. In her absence, and as though to increase the interest of the day, someone had turned up driving a rather special old-time motor bike and sidecar; it was painted yellow and bore the flamboyant initials AA, signifying the Automobile Association. As a young lady, said Hannah, she had ridden pillion behind an uncle who owned a motor bike. On another occasion, she was offered a lift on a motor bike as she walked down the dale, but declined. "I might have done something daft like leaning the wrong way so that it wouldn't be easy to steer."

ON THE FARM

In 1992, I joined Hannah and fifty friends on a tour of Bowsber Farm, near Clapham. Hannah recalled her own farming days in Baldersdale; she was bemused by such new-fangled features as milking parlours, undercover lambing pens and motorised shepherding. She patted a collie, fondled some lively pups and drank tea from a plastic cup. Hannah arrived at Bowsber with friends from Abbot Hall. Those friends included Mrs Lavinia Thwaites, a good friend of Hannah's from Cotherstone, and members of the Abbot Hall staff.

It was one of those damp, half-lit days which a dalesman had in mind when he said: "Day looks as if it's bin up all neet." The limestone scars near Clapham had lost their silvery sheen. Curlews, newly arrived from the coast, couldn't be bothered to go through their song-glide routine. At the dairy farm, only the dogs were lively. Hannah, unchanged by all the media fuss of recent years, but recoiling from photographic flashbulbs because of her delicate sight, was reticent about stroking a chain-rattling dog, even though it rested its forepart on the bar of a fence and occasionally held its head on one side in a most engaging way.

"I'm daft over dogs," said Hannah, "but it's just as well to be wary. If he takes a jump over that railing I don't know how he'll land up." She warmed to the collie pups, two black-and-white and two brown-and-white, which she pronounced to be

Great Aunt's straw bonnet.

"fine puppies" and "lovely". She also had an instant rapport with a lamb that stood in an arc of light and heat from an electric lamp. The lambs she saw had "bonnie complexions".

It was the first time she had set foot in limestone country. Being a guest at Abbot Hall, she had left her trusty wellies back at Cotherstone. Farming at Bowsber was on a much bigger scale than she was accustomed to and the milk cattle – a Friesian/Holstein cross – were much larger than her Balderstone "beefers".

I tracked down Hannah to the outbuilding where the collie pups were in a pen of generous size. I recalled that the last time I had seen her on a farm, it had been Low Birk Hatt; she had been hand-raking hay at the top of a meadow, wearing Great Aunt's straw bonnet. "I still have that bonnet," she told me. Hannah did not visit the large cattle shed, commenting: "It's not my kind of farming, though I do drink milk."

I asked her if she missed farming. Hannah said, instantly, "There's a time for everything. I don't miss going out in all weathers – and being on the go all the time, no matter what you feel like. It's a good life when you are young and in good health." My last glimpse of Hannah that day came just before the visitors departed in their large bus. She was drinking tea out of a plastic cup and then eating a large scone. Hannah looked thoughtful; she was doubtless thinking about Low Birk Hatt and about Rosa, her favourite cow.

Keen to have a farmer's assessment of Hannah's farming at Low Birk Hatt, I chatted with John Geldard, retired farmer, who often visited Low Birk Hatt with his wife Margaret. How would he sum up Hannah as a farmer? He thought for a little while, then observed: "In no way could you say she was a really knowledgeable farmer. But she was a happy one. It was her life – and she loved it. She loved animals; she loved looking after them. Profit was not the main thing about it. If she had been keen on making a big profit, she would have farmed differently. She would have had more stock on the land and some more regular help."

John, who farmed for many years at Malham, in the Craven limestone country, added: "Hannah struggled on in a way that enabled her to manage the farm by herself. The result from it as a farm was not really good enough but, nevertheless, it was a pleasure to go and see her. She really did enjoy life." In 1980, Malham Show Committee thought it would be a nice idea if they invited Hannah to come to the show as chief guest. She agreed to come, though – as ever – was determined not to make a speech. She would answer questions.

The farmer who volunteered to collect her from Baldersdale knew he must be back at the showfield before luncheon began at noon. When he reached Low Birk Hatt, Hannah was in the bath. He had to wait a while. Hannah emerged, smartly dressed, and they managed to get back to the showfield in time. Her appearance, her bright face and "lovely white hair", impressed those attending the show. Hannah, courtesy of Yorkshire Television, had become fashionable in her attire during trips abroad.

John and Margaret, asked to chaperone Hannah for the duration of Malhamdale Show, watched her perform various duties, such as picking out what she considered to be the best-looking sheepdog from a line-up. A queue formed of people who had books they wished to have autographed or simply to have a few words with her. Hannah, in thanking the Geldards, said: "I would like you to call on me sometime." John knew the area where she lived but not the precise location of the farm. "So we called on a farmer whose house was by the main road. He said the direct road to Low Birk Hatt was grown up and the bridge broken down. There was a way round by the reservoir."

It was quite a nice day, so they walked down the old route, noticing the situation of the farmhouse on an elevated position where land rose from the eastern shore of a reservoir. There were springs on the land which, to John, an experienced farmer, was in need of improvement. "It was starting to grow rushes. And it wanted draining. The land was not stocked adequately for the size of it." The meadows were reasonably good. The pastures were "rough", with much bent, a coarse form of sheep-resistant grass.

Hannah was happy tending eight cows – Shorthorns, which she raised for beef. They were in excellent condition. "We are talking back a few years now when Shorthorns were about. Dales farmers gradually went into Ayrshires and then into Friesians. Hannah's stock were not sold as dairy cows. She couldn't have managed to milk seven cows and, anyway, couldn't have done anything with the milk."

When the Geldards arrived at Low Birk Hatt, Hannah came to the door. "She was in her old and tattered clothing. She had a peculiar stick; it wasn't a proper farmer's stick but part of the branch of a tree. She took us to see the source of her water – a spring – and said that in winter she had to break the ice." The visitors could see the water bubbling slightly. She would ladle water into a bucket. The

Over: There was always a close bond between Hannah and her cattle, which were kept in good condition and treated like pets.

cows had to be let out to drink in winter; she had no water bowls. "They had been brought up in a way that she could tell them what to do – and they'd do it. She had a dog but it was not a particularly good one with stock."

Hannah related that when she began to farm here, her parents were alive. On their death, and that of an uncle, she had been left to carry on alone. She showed John Geldard her cattle and especially her favourite cow Rosa, putting her arm affectionately round its neck. There was such a bond between Hannah and her animals. In summertime, the cattle did not take much looking after. They were looking after themselves. But in winter she had to get up to attend to them.

Cows do not normally drink until they have had some hay – that gives them a thirst – so she had a system of feeding them before they drank. And then she'd let them out for water. It took her almost all day, because they were usually watered twice a day. John was keen to know how she went on when the time came for selling some of the stock. Said Hannah: "I'm only in a very small way now. I really only sell one or two cows a year." She sent them to Kirkby Stephen auction mart; a neighbour looked after the selling side.

The cattle were in good condition. Just like pets. A bit on the heavy side. There was no suggestion there had been very good breeding. But they were good, heavy Shorthorn types. In haytime, this vital winter fodder was secured and baled on her behalf by neighbouring farmers.

For a few years when she was on her own the house was tidy. Then things got on the top of her, to quote a Dales saying. Hannah had two televisions. One had no picture. The other had no sound. The Geldards were impressed by her knowledge of things that were happening in the world. What they remembered about the living room was a mass of parcels underneath the table. Some came from London and contained wine. Most of the parcels were unopened. One or two of them were two or three years back. She had a long sofa that was covered with junk.

On another occasion, Hannah was anxious. The day before a cow had given birth to a calf. She had the calf inside the house. She was worried, having detected signs of inflammation. She asked John what he thought about the calf's condition. He replied: "I think you should have a vet." As the years progressed, the Geldards managed to get round to the house with a car.

There was never any suggestion of us interfering with Hannah's work. It was always: "Come in. Sit down." Once you got in there it was difficult to get away without being rude. "We didn't have a cup of tea because it would be a big job for her; it took her a long time to make tea because she was talking in among making it." In a walk round the farm with their friends, the Birtwhistles of Bordley, a photograph was taken of them standing against a gates that was "all tied up with binder twine. I don't think you could have opened it; it would not have held together."

In 1985, John Geldard retired from farming. "We visited Hannah with the news. Oh, have you. Oh, Mr Geldard" – she could never bring herself to call me John – "that's what I'll have to do, but I don't know how to start." John replied: "It won't be a big job for you. Whatever you want, just say and some of us will give you a hand."

At the next meeting, when he tried to move things forward, Hannah had changed her mind. Eventually, a sale was put in hand, with Gordon Pratt, of Hawes, as the auctioneer. On days prior to Sale Day, there were bonfires, fed with unwanted things from the house, among such items being many years accumulation of newspapers. Quite a lot of things she said she could not part with. They thought she was keeping far more than she needed. Which she was. An old, torn sofa and a huge table went for good sums. There was more than one four-poster bed.

"I took Gordon up one day to give him an idea of the fields. Hannah hadn't wanted an auction. She was keen to know who would get the land. "We valued it all. And blow me, if Hannah didn't go off the idea once again, delaying things for another year." It was eventually decided to put the land up for tender, with John invited to Hawes for the opening of the tenders. Two of three lots were bought by an organisation who were keen to improve it, then let it out.

On the night before Sale Day, the proceedings were to be held in the open air, the weather being cool and damp, the ground wet. What were involved were the house and effects, tools, etc. A good home had been found for the cattle. As bidding developed, Hannah stood a little apart, but in earshot. If you went to her, she did not want to talk. Emotionally, it was a hard day for her.

That morning she had said: "Mr Geldard, there's something I would like to give you." She had several stone troughs. "You may pick one of them." It was a nice gesture of appreciation but John could not take it up, having no suitable method of transportation.

It wasn't a particularly long sale, all parcels having been dispersed. People could wander through the house, even going upstairs, where the now famous four-poster bed had been.

Hannah and a group of friends out in the broad expanses of Upper Teesdale.

HANNAH'S COUNTRY

Her preference is for in-between country – tracts of land that were neither unduly cultivated nor excessively wild. Hannah is inclined to shudder at the sight of lofty mountains, layered with snow. Natural spectacles, such as Cauldron Snout in Upper Teesdale and Cautley Spout, on the steep side of the Howgill Fells, appeal to her. So does a small village – Brough, for instance, which is mainly two rows of building separated by a wide expanse of road, or quaint little Cartmel near Morecambe Bay. Hannah remembers Cartmel Methodist Church because of a capacity attendance when she was speaking. The chairman had to sit on the floor.

1 – BIRTHPLACE OF THE RIVER TEES

The head of Teesdale is broad, with peat and heather and a reservoir where once a natural lake was frequented in summer by farm-bred geese. Cross Fell, which at 2,930-ft is the highest point on the Pennines, dominates a wild scene and is reflected in the reservoir on rare calm days. The source of the mighty Tees is, at 2,500-ft, not much lower than the summit plateau of Cross Fell. The river was once the border between Yorkshire and county Durham, with Westmorland having a slice near the dalehead. Durham now claims it all. The upper valley of the Tees has been declared an Area of Outstanding Natural Beauty for the Northern Pennines.

This is The Big Country, an area for superlatives and a district in which Hannah can feel at home. Characterful people inhabit a valley characterised by outcropping basalt, whitewashed farms and moorland sheep. For many years, the dale-farmers have managed their inby lands and turned out their sheep to summer on the outby areas where the land is elevated and unimproved. The bonnie heather blooms on dry ridges and the hollows are lagged with sphagnum.

Between 1600 and 1900 a duel economy was practised. Lead mining employed a large male labour force. On the hill farms, it was customary for men who were mining to stay from home on weekdays, leaving the care of the farms to women and young people. Dalesfolk regulated their environment to ensure it was not grossly abused. The Teesdale commons were stinted, a stint representing the pasturage of a sheep. The term acre has little meaning on the felltops where the state of the ground varies and there is much outcropping rock. At one time you might find "dry" cows on the commons, each beast representing several stints.

In the upper valley of the Tees, farmers have their wits tested by climatic excesses – though very hot days are rare. It is an area of low temperatures, of high rainfall and much snow in winter. The growing season in some years seems to be little more than a good-natured wink between the rigours of spring and autumn. At Cow Green, towards the end of August, the temperature recorded was a minus three degrees centigrade.

Winter might be long and hard, overstaying its welcome until May. At the head of Teesdale, an east wind in February tends to bring snow that is crisp and even. It literally squeaks underfoot. The blizzards that raged in these parts in 1946-7 and 1962-3 put down snow that lay, in each period, for about eight weeks. In February, 1929, High Force, normally a tumultuous waterfall, was frozen into stillness.

Farms in the upper valley of the Tees were built of limestone, with some whinstone: the walls might be up to two feet thick. Alas, some were damp, the stone being porous. No deadening uniformity exists in the type of building to be seen. Part of the enchantment of the area is in the architectural variety, yet unity is preserved by the white walls, especially on the Raby estate, where cobs of lime, the means to whiten a building, were distributed and the farmers encouraged to do the work themselves. Some farms sit behind shelter-belts of trees that protect them from the prevailing wind, which is a south-westerly.

Hannah, visiting relatives or friends in the upper dale, would notice that a dam was being built, this being to regulate the water and ensure there was a flow during the dry season. The impounded water covered Cow Green, where smallholders used to summer their cattle. As noted, geese were pastured; then, waddling down a gentle slope, they might swim in the Weel, where the river was deep and slow-moving. Greensward was known to be good for tups, hardening

Juniper is especially associated with Upper Teesdale and is one of many plants that make the area such an attraction for botanists.

them up. Tom Buffey, the site research officer, whom I met in the summer of 1970, when the dam was under construction, was impressed by Teesdale's transient conditions.

He said: "When there's a clear day, the early morning and evening are the most beautiful. The sun throws long shadows across the hags and vegetation; there's a variety of colouring – red, chestnut, brown, green, black – changing all the time. Add to this the shadows of fast-moving clouds and you do not have the same conditions for five minutes at a time." Work on the dam virtually stopped from November to April.

To the naturalist, Teesdale is associated especially with flowers. Speckling a tract of sugar-limestone on Widdybank Fell is an assemblage of wild plants unique in the land. The list is long and, to a botanist, exciting, including spring gentian, a speck of deep blue contrasting with the faded vegetation round about, purple mountain pansy, vernal sandwort, which has tiny, white, star-shaped flowers, and yellow mountain saxifrage. Here, too, is the bird's eye primrose (*Primula farinosa*), its flowers a delicate pink and its leaves of an unusual pastel green, smooth above and mealy white beneath. Botanists also rejoice when they see some of Teesdale's herby meadows – a rarity in themselves on the Pennines now that silage-making has been taken up on a grand scale.

Today, a car park lies within an arrow-shot of the reservoir. From this park, a hard path extends through what used to be a wilderness, populated by astonishingly tame red grouse and by golden plover that have a melancholic whistle. The path leads to Cauldron Snout, a turbulent flow of water down a natural staircase formed of basalt, the durable whin sill. Wherever it obtrudes, the scenery is spectacular, as at the most impressive stretches of the Roman Wall and, a seaward termination, the Farne Isles off the Northumbrian coast.

The concrete section of the dam has horizontal and vertical jointing to reflect the structure of the rocks at Cauldron Snout, the overflow, which races down a staircase of unyielding rock. The Snout is also on the line of the Pennine Way, which is Britain's second longest continuous footpath, extending from Edale in Derbyshire to Kirk Yetholm in Scotland. The Snout was described by the novelist William Riley as having a fierceness that he had not found in any other. Riley, writing long before the dam was built, added that the sense of contrast had something to do with it – "the quiet, cataleptic river roused to sudden frothing madness."

A solitary farm, Birkdale, is tucked away in the valley between Cauldron Snout and High Cup Nick. It stands in isolation, yet everywhere there is evidence of human activity – buildings and walls, mines and old tracks used by packhorse traffic. The first time I took the road to Birkdale Farm the road was a rutted track between tussocks of ling. Sir Clement Jones, when visiting the area in 1947, noticed that in the absence of a road the tenant farmer travelled on horseback when visiting shops at the distant village. Now, observed Sir Clement, times had changed.

Mr Airey, the farmer he met those long years ago, had a tractor and was "bumping and squelching and skidding about over the boggy ground [on his way to get supplies] between his house and the road." He had a house-cow – actually two cows, plus a calf – but intended to get rid of the cows and "go over to tinned stuff." (The owner of Birkdale Farm arranged for a good road to be made in 1959).

My favourite story of Birkdale – an ancient tale - is about the day of Granny's funeral. Birkdale was in the Westmorland outback yet the parish church was at Dufton, in the Eden Valley. So that is where the body of Granny was to be taken, strapped to the back of a fell pony that followed a track through wild country,

The lonely farm of Birkdale, hidden in the valley between Cauldron Snout and High Cup Nick.

including the rim of High Cup Nick. Tearful grandchildren, who remained at the farm with a carer, waved her off. On arriving at Dufton, with time to spare, the mourners visited the local inn. The pony slipped its halter and returned to Birkdale Farm, where the excited children were reported as saying: "Granny's coming back again."

I recall long chats with the Bainbridge family, residents at Birkdale when their nearest neighbours were at Peghorn Farm, a good four miles away. In 1985, Brian Bainbridge told me he had walked half-bred sheep to Appleby by way of High Cup Nick, which a shepherd boy described as "a greeart goolf." Sharing the high grazings near Birkdale were sheep from some East Fellside farmers, at Dufton and Hilton. If the winter was "open", Birkdale sheep were left on the fell. Gathering took place several times a year, for lambing, dipping and spaining [the separation of lambs from their mothers].

As with Hannah, at her remote little farm, it was the winter that tested the resolution of the occupants at Birkdale. The Airey family were in residence during the 1947 snowstorms. The farmer, who had begun the winter with around 700 sheep, lost all but 45 and they reared only seven lambs.

Sir Clement Jones, chatting with the Airey family just after that terrible winter, heard that at the height of the storm the provisions at the farm were almost exhausted. The farmer's sister had just cooked what she thought would be their last griddle cake, and she and her brother were sitting down to eat it when, "as though in some story from the Old Testament, there arrived (like ravens) to the farm two men on skis who had set out from Middleton-in-Teesdale bringing a supply of groceries and other food."

In 1962, the Bainbridges started the winter with some 400 ewes. They were in the process of building up the flock. Snow fell and the ground became an undulating white desert. On the clear, sunny, bitterly cold days that followed, three-quarters of the flock perished. That springtime, there was an unnatural quietness about Birkdale. Scarcely a sheep bleated. Much more recently, snow came out of a clear sky in April. "It was a lovely day on the Thursday but by Friday morning we got up to find it was snowing. By dinner-time a blizzard was raging and visibility was zero."

The sheep, shocked by the impact of the storm, and by some recent injections they had been given, decided to lamb all at once. "They were dropping lambs in the snow...We put them in the buildings and we had a house full of lambs. I was taking milk out of a ewe and feeding any lamb, just to keep it going. And all the time I was thinking: what if the ewes don't take to their lambs when conditions improve?" The ewes and lambs were turned out – and almost all of them were re-united."

Mickle Fell, which blocks out the western sky when you traverse Birkdale, was prior to local government reorganisation in 1974 regarded (proudly) as the attic of Yorkshire. Mickle Fell (2,591ft) is a hump on the great slab of high country lying to the north of the road between Brough and Middleton-in-Teesdale. Up there, in what must surely be England's last great wilderness, it tends to play second fiddle to Cross Fell, which lies a little to the north.

Master-faults gave this northern Pennine area a special isolation, which the passing years, and man's steadily increasing dominance of the landscape, has not removed. There is no easy way to the summit of Mickle Fell until, and heaven

The curlew, widely regarded as a harbinger of spring, is a favourite of Hannah.

forbid, you have access with a helicopter. Wandering in this area is chancy. Dozens of signs mark the periphery of an Army training area that sprawls over 40,000 acres. It was prepared for use during the second world war at a cost of millions of pounds.

Mickle Fell, approached from the west, crowns the horizon as a big, smooth lump, rising only a few hundred feet from the high Pennine landscape. It has beauty of a kind, but this is a soft, almost pastoral beauty. There is none of the savage grandeur one might have expected from the highest point in what was then England's largest county.

You must grant Mickle Fell distinction as a viewpoint. All around it are the bare ridges of the Pennines, resembling waves in a petrified sea. On my first visit, from the Westmorland side, I saw the remains of an RAF bomber that crashed during the Second World War. Inside, resting on the frame of the aircraft, was a row of old ring ouzel nests, here protected from the wild whims of the weather. Eventually, the remains of the big aircraft were moved from the fell to a place where it might be preserved – and revered.

Hannah grew up in her little Pennine dale with the voices of moor birds near

High Force marks the end of the dramatic reaches of Upper Teesdale. It has many moods, ranging from white fury to relative calm.

at hand. In Teesdale, wide expanses of heather suits the golden plover, a trim bird with scimitar wings which returns to these vast moors as early as February. For nesting, they seek out the drier parts of the open moor where the vegetation is sparse. A golden plover likes all-round visibility. The far-reaching alarm note – tiu - has been likened to the sound made when opening a rusty gate.

The curlew, a large streaky-brown bird with a long, down-curved beak, is a favourite of Hannah, for the curlew brings the moors back to life with its bubbling call. When a crow approaches a curlew's territory, the sentry bird dives on it with a loud call and pulls out of its dive in a whoosh of displaced air. In early spring, cock lapwings tumble through the air as though intent on dashing themselves against the ground, pulling out of the dive at the last minute. Some people know the bird as "flopwing".

Grouse-shooting is part of the Upper Teesdale economy. A poor season, and the fact that no shooting took place, would have a knock-on effect on the economy. Local folk are employed as beaters on the moors. In the 1980s, when I last inquired into the economics of grouse-shooting, I was told: "If you have only twenty-five beaters a day, and you shoot for twenty-five days, and supposing you earn £10 a head per day, it represents quite a lot of money going into the local purse."

Where does Upper Teesdale end? For me, it is the 70-ft waterfall known as High Force. The river has had plenty of ground – some eighteen miles – to build up power before it takes a leap from a rim of basalt into a deep plunge-pool. The time to visit High Force, a waterfall of many moods, is when there is a sudden thaw and the snow is melting on Cross Fell and its remote Pennine neighbours. A single mighty fall on what was once the Yorkshire side of the river becomes two falls as the Durham channel fills and overflows. Then High Force is in a white fury. With water spreading turbulently from bank to bank it resembles Niagara. Yet when the rain stops, the river level falls quickly and you wonder what all the fuss has been about.

Most of us see the valley in summer, when conditions are benign. The sun shines. A light haze forms – and the whitewashed farms of Teesdale, north of the river, stand out dreamy-white against lush meadows.

2 – THE HEART OF EDENVALE

Hannah's visit to a flower festival in Mallerstang and overnight stay at a cottage near the summit of the Settle-Carlisle railway, in the Pennine dale-country, was an introduction to the valley down which the River Eden flows. The river in Hannah's native dale run south; but the Eden flowed northwards, passing through a limestone ravine called Hell Gill – the word hell relating to a cave - beyond which it scoured a rocky bed in Mallerstang, then flowed grandly down a widening valley to Carlisle and the sea.

The name Eden relates to water, not to paradise, though this broad vale seems like the other Eden when matched against the blue-greys of the Lakeland fells to the west and the tawny Pennine uplift to the east. If Hannah had entrained at Settle for Carlisle, she would have been aware of passing from the limestone grey of North Ribblesdale and Mallerstang to the sandstone redness of much of the Eden Valley.

New Red Sandstone, formed in desert-like conditions, and the gold of ripening corn, gives summertime Eden Vale a most colourful aspect. Hannah, touring the Eden Valley, would be captivated not by topography but by people. A solitary person, content with her own company, Hannah occasionally – not often - revelled in being one of a crowd. It happened gloriously when she attended a garden party at Buckingham Palace.

There was an assembly of dalesfolk in Mallerstang on the festival day. The Weather Clerk was in a happy mood. Visitors to the little church passed between floral displays and entered a building where, for the moment, flowers distracted attention from a range of attractively embroidered footrests. In the Eden Valley, where farming is still a dominant feature, Hannah – on that summer's day – recaptured the delights of her little farm in Baldersdale. She grew up when the meadow grass was cut and sun-dried, as opposed to the modern idea of cutting, wilting, then silage-making.

Hannah mentioned to me the frustrating seasons when, with the onset of rain, the hay was piked, set in great heaps, smoothed and rounded at the top. At the age of seventeen, Hannah had forked hay into a hole set high above the ground so that someone just inside the barn might collect and position it neatly on the mewstead. "I liked that," said Hannah. "If only I had some of the strength and energy now that I had then. In my young days, there didn't seem to be any limit to it." Yet when she had glanced at father's account books, and had seen how sparse were the financial returns from much hard work, she had wondered how he managed to keep the farm viable.

Appleby, in a loop of the River Eden, is an old town full of historical associations, from a venerable castle and an ancient estate, at the top and bottom of a broad street known as Boroughgate. Appleby has two prominent white crosses, one near the castle gates, the other in the lower part of the street where markets took place. Appleby respects the memory of the forthright Lady Anne Clifford, who had her name engraved on all her bountiful works.

She was born in Skipton Castle, being taken away from the town at the age of nine and in the company of her parents and brother. When she returned in 1605, to belatedly take over the northern estates, she was an imposing person who, despite frequent illnesses, two marriages and excessive child-bearing, had kept her good looks..

In her younger days, Lady Anne had been small and dainty, with black eyes, quick and lively, and brown hair that – when combed out – reached to the calves of her legs. With good tutors, titled relatives and a devoted and devout mother, Anne was familiar with the Court of Queen Elizabeth. Her introduction came when, aged thirteen, she came through the influence of a titled aunt, this being Ann Countess of Warwick. Anne, when young, attended the court of Queen Elizabeth. She was subsequently familiar with the lively, elaborate rounds of the Court of King James and Queen Anne as one of the Queen's ladies-in-waiting. Anne and her mother were present when her father – the wayward, buccaneering

Kirkby Stephen, gateway to Mallerstang, has strong links with Lady Anne Clifford.

FOUNTAINS YARD

SATAN IN BONDS

THE BUTTER MARKET

OLD GRAMMAR SCHOOL AND PARISH CHURCH

KIRKBY STEPHEN

George Clifford – died "penitently, willing and Christianly", as Anne confided in her dairy.

Mother and daughter fought the terms of father's will, which ignored Anne as next of kin, favouring the next male in line. Eventually, on his death, Anne could come into her own and move North. She and a "good and pious mother" enjoyed each other's company to the extent that when mother died Anne erected a commemorative pillar at the roadside, about a quarter of a mile south of Brougham Castle, one of her northern possessions. Typically, she also left an annuity of four pounds for the poor of the parish, the money to be distributed every year on April 2, the actual day of the last parting.

Dr C G Williamson, in his biography, summed up Lady Anne as being studious and bookish, devout, stately, solemn and grave. She was admittedly a Royalist and had her foibles – a passion for her family and for rules of precedence in rank; but also she possessed an intense love of the country. She was extremely generous to guests, friends and tenants, and she wore simple country clothes ('not disliked by any, but copied by none') so to have the more to give away.

"Taking into consideration the position to which she was born and viewing

Market day in Boroughgate, Appleby – an old town full of historical associations.

her against a background of the times," wrote Williamson, "I cannot but feel that both the seventeenth century and posterity would have been the poorer without her. Lest I be misunderstood, let me say that I do not write from the viewpoint of who she was but from a wish to make a fair estimate of her character."

The castle at Appleby, ruined since 1569, was defended during the Civil Wars, surrendered, then slighted in 1648. Lady Anne restored it despite an edict that such a thing should never happen. Cromwell, who was keen to keep the castles in a ruined state, must have admired her fortitude. No one was permitted to intervene as she turned back the clock to the medieval period in her building style. A small army of masons, joiners and lead-beaters worked on the tower. New floors were fitted. The roof was raised to eighty feet and covered in lead.

Her Ladyship now had a viewpoint from which to survey a much-loved Pennine panorama. The castle has not been open to the public in recent times. The last time I climbed the tower was on a crisp, sunlit day when, looking eastwards to the Pennines, I clearly saw the great gash of High Cup Nick. Anne restored St Lawrence's church, which stands on a site hallowed by Christians since Danish times. Lady Anne was interred within its grey walls.

Anne, last of the Cliffords, died at about six o'clock in the evening of March 22, 1676. Her funeral took place at Appleby on April 14. Her body, in a close-fitting shroud of lead (there was no coffin as such) was placed on a rough stone bench immediately under her elaborate monument, which she had commissioned to be made in her lifetime. The coats of arms on her tomb collectivelty formed an early Debrett.

In addition to being Countess Dowager of Pembroke, Dorset and Montgomery, daughter and heir of the 3rd Earl of Cumberland, she was Baroness Clifford, Westmorland and Vescy, Lady of the Honour of Skipton-in-Craven and High Sheriff of Westmorland. Anne Clifford is dead but her spirit lives on, not least in the almshouses she had built at Appleby. When, in recent times, it was decided that an electrical supply should be provided here, an old lady – one of the so-called sisters – wondered if Lady Anne would mind.

What Lady Anne thought of the New Fair and the intrusion of travellers with horses and hooped wagons is not recorded. At least, I have not seen such a record. Hannah, a lover of old customs, would doubtless approve. Appleby Fair is ancient, receiving its charter from James II in June 1685. The name New Fair came into use when the Gregorian calendar was established in 1752 and the traditional dates for the fair are the second Wednesday in June and the preceding day.

Travellers who converge on the 32-acre domed Fair Hill, formerly Gallows Hill, in early June, have long outnumbered those reared in strict Romany traditions. Most travellers arrive in motor vehicles towing large caravans. Others adopt the leisurely course of their forebears, with traditional wagons drawn by horses – piebalds for preference. The journey might take several days. At night, drawn off the road, the horses are staked out and graze the verges while meals are cooked for the by now weary travellers.

The fame of the New Fair has rested mainly on horse-dealing. Yet horses are not referred to in the charter. Celebrity animals, known as "gipsy cobs", are black and white or brown and white. Attempts were made in the mid-1960s to have the fair closed down. A reprieve was granted following pressure from some influential people, including a member of the Lowther family. Gallows Hill came available at modest charge, being provided with a piped water supply and latrines.

When I first visited Appleby New Fair in 1964, the streets of the little town held a concourse of cars, vans, lorries and horse-drawn carts being driven by travellers, whose faces radiated pride and pleasure. Cigar-smoking men handling wads of banknotes with a casual air were invading the shops. In the cafes, ample helpings of fish, eggs, peas and chips were being tucked away.

A family from Shelf, near Bradford, who had a hooped caravan, arrived in Appleby via Harrogate and Boroughbridge; they left the Great North Road at Scotch Corner and crossed Stainmore into the Eden Valley. The daily mileage was from ten to fifteen, but they did not force too hard a pace for fear of lathering the horses with sweat, the weather being close. This outing was one of their main holidays. "When we get home, we'll have been on the road for about five weeks."

St Lawrence's church, Appleby, was restored by Lady Anne Clifford and is her last resting place.

Caravans stretched in long, almost unbroken lines along the roadside towards Long Marton. The hooped wagons were blurred to sight as blue smoke rose from campfires. The contents of the travellers' vans were exposed to popular gaze, for on show days every status symbol, including the best china, was on show. Crown Derby was especially prized for its colour. A proud owner said: "We are little Egyptians; we don't like white. Crown Derby is pretty, colourful and decorative." It is bought to display and also as a durable investment.

Strident voices – oy, oy, oy – were to be heard above the sound of pounding hooves as horses were displayed before potential buyers. The action of running a horse up and down created excitement. After several runs, the horse was halted, a small crowd gathered and bidding began. In a few minutes the price climbed so rapidly that a still perspiring horse had changed hands three or four times. A fat roll of money was produced in a deal that ended with a hand-slap.

The celebrated Brough Hill Fair, held on a roadside site between Appleby and the village of Brough, evolved from one established by Charter granted by Edward III to Robert de Clifford in 1329. The original venue, Brough Intack, was changed to the Hill in about 1661 following an outbreak of plague. Brough Hill burgeoned after 1752, with the growth of cattle-droving from Scotland in a season that began in May and reached its peak in the autumn. By the early part of the nineteenth century, when cattle and sheep as well as horses were changing hands, it was rated as one of the largest fairs in the north country.

As Brough Hill was mainly a horse fair, the animals were driven in from a wide area. There were farm horses, light horses and ponies. For some of the young people it was a time for romance. Courtship that began at the New Fair at Appleby continued at Brough. Elopements were fairly common. Eventually, marriages between travellers conformed with those in ordinary society. Those arranged at Brough were quietly solemnised at Penrith Registry Office.

Jonty Wilson, blacksmith at Kirkby Lonsdale for many years, and a considerable horseman, told me that a man who bought a horse from one of the sharp-witted travellers at Brough Hill should have experienced every trick in the book or he would be cheated. I recorded Jonty's life and times in a booklet published in 1978. Brough Hill Fair was an event he knew well.

Jonty told me: "Brough was the Mecca of farmers and breeders, dealers and gypsies, tinkers and hustlers and all the hangers-on and the rag-tag and bobtail of the horse world from the four corners of Britain. The Romany clans came from as far afield as the Forest of Dean, the wilds of Wales and the Scottish Highlands – a colourful procession of odd-coloured horses, shining brass work and gaily decorated caravans winding their way leisurely to the fair, hawking the villages and towns en route with their wares and indulging in a spot of fortune-telling as a prosperous sideline. At night, their camp fires could be seen twinkling on every wayside clearing and bit of moorland.

When attending the Hill, Jonty heard of a farmer who fancied something a bit more sprightly and took his 18-year-old mare to the fair. He sold her and searched diligently for something with appeal. Eventually he bought the same mare in the evening, not recognising it, for now it was hogged, trimmed and doctored, offered as an eight-year old jet black at double the selling price – guaranteed by the vendor as "the best of her colour in Mother England."

A buyer who asked for the usual "bit o' luck" on the purchase price was told: "Nay, lad, I cannot give you any brass, but I'll throw in another horse – for luck.."

3 – SEDBERGH AND THE HOWGILLS

The road up Lunesdale from Kirkby Lonsdale to Sedbergh is flanked by hedges that owe their height and luxuriance to something more than the disinclination of farmers to trim them. Mild weather filters up from the Irish Sea and there is a high humidity in the valley. With such a climate the telegraph poles are apt to sprout. It is in marked contrast with the upper dales known especially to Hannah, though each type of landscape has its appeal.

One tends to keep an eye on the road, which has an aversion to going straight for long. Few drivers are aware of the Roman milestone in a field near Middleton – a milestone which for many years was buried and scarred by ploughshares. The owner had it removed and re-positioned. It is now a short distance from the route the Romans blazed from Over Burrow and through the Lune Gorge to Brougham in the Eden Valley.

On the approach to the Lune bridge, the road is shadowed by trees. The bridge is at an acute angle and its narrowness ensures that motorists slow almost to snail's pace, checking on other road users, before crossing. Sedbergh has a splendid backdrop in the lofty hummocks of the Howgills – rounded, slaty hills that appeal to visitors and are the all-the-year-round grazing area for Rough Fell sheep. Also, one might add, the dark-toned fell ponies that are sure-footed enough to stay upright on the steepest ground. Some ponies find winter grazing and shelter near Cautley Spout to the east of the range.

In a hot spell, the Howgills tend to get browned off. As a farmer put it: "There's not a lot of soil up there. The land needs a regular wetting." The men who run stock on the Howgills are not accustomed to undue feather-bedding. The hard nature of their lives shows in their faces and finds a reflection in their manners. Fell farmers are naturally cautious and shrewd.

Administratively, Sedbergh when I first knew it was out on a limb, being a good sixty-five miles from Wakefield, the county town prior to 1974. At a time when UDI was a major talking point, the initials meaning Universal Declaration of Independence, I was told that Sedbergh was ideally placed for this to happen. Said a local official: "There's a very narrow bridge on every approach road. All we need to do is to blow up those bridges and we'd be completely isolated."

By-passing the town, I followed a road to Lowgill. It was almost like being in a leafy tunnel, though for a short spell the view opened out and I saw the sunlit Howgills at their most imposing. It's a view that provides a dramatic backcloth to the M6 in the Lune Gorge. Years ago, chatting with the merry miller at Lowgill, his premises being just beyond one of the arches of the redundant Lowgill railway viaduct, I was told of modifications carried out to a new lorry to enable it to cross a nearby bridge over the Lune.

That bridge, high arched and narrow, like a rainbow set in stone, would not have taken the lorry as it was delivered. Its width had to be lessened if it was to cross the bridge without slurring. Recently, when I asked about traffic on the hedge-blanketed road system beyond, I was told: "You'll be all right. Road'll be clear. Postman's just been!" He would be somewhere ahead, attuned to the local constrictions.

Howgill, the tiny settlement after which the Fells were named, is screened by trees part way along a narrow, hedge-flanked road that runs between Sedbergh and Tebay. Relief is provided for travellers, and good parking places for walkers intent on bagging some Howgills, by a stretch of open road on the flanks of the fells. Part of the Roman road system – there was a fort in the gorge – is known as the Fair Mile, from which many walkers gain their operational elevation when bagging some of the fells. Others park here for a view of the Lune gorge, with traffic on the ever-busy M6 and the Lancaster-Carlisle railway to provide diversions from the grand scenery.

The local stretch of the motorway was built at a cost of £12m. When it was first opened, and local people were in the process of becoming used to the noise, a farmer told me that at sheep gathering time on the fellside beyond, the rising noise from the motorway was so intense his dog could not hear all his whistled commands.

Work went on continuously, in twelve-hour shifts, a process that began when the contractors built a six-mile access road along which moved special equipment, over 250 items of large plant, including 35-ton Euclid trucks. Twenty bridges were needed. Three of them were each valued at over half a million pounds. One of the 19 box culverts was to be three-quarters of a mile long. A local man thought the motorway enhanced the view, adding, "The Gorge always looked austere, cold."

I first explored the Sedbergh area in the 1960s when, according to a local man, the town was half dead for most of the time and fully dead on Thursday, when the shops closed early. He was being less than fair to what was then a mile-long, 400-yards wide town. On market day, when farm folk converge on Sedbergh, a countrygoer like Hannah would realise that an income from farming is still an important aspect of local commercial life. The farmers support a variety of local businesses. Observing life on the farm round about the town is of great interest to visitors.

No-one is sure when the gh was added to form the name Sedbergh. Old maps and the plate that belongs to St Andrew's Church gives the name as Sedber. Local people are apt to say they live in Sebber town. The 700-year-old charter of Sedbergh specifies Thursday, but now the market is held on Wednesday.

Sedbergh is a long, narrow, compact town. Its main thoroughfare was hopelessly inadequate for modern traffic, especially a spate of summer holiday traffic between the populous North East and the Lancashire resorts of Blackpool and Morecambe. At one point, the main street is only about eleven feet wide. A one-way traffic system ensures there is a measure of order.

Sedberghian relates to a resident and also gives a title to the magazine published at Sedbergh School. The school, old and demanding of space, is largely responsible for the modern shape of the town and its semi-rural aspects. The school buildings are not in a huddle, as with many schools, but lie with broad green spaces between them. There are a dozen rugby fields. A huge cricket field near the Church ensures that the old part of town is not hemmed in by buildings.

Sedbergh School evolved into one of the finest of its kind in the North. It gives prestige, fame and fortune to the town. The academic development dates mainly from the early part of the nineteenth century. There is bound to be mental liveliness in the town generally when a large number of highly-qualified teachers and several hundred serious-minded pupils live here.

When I saw the lads about town in 1962, their uniform was known as the blues, with good reason, for a boy wore blue shorts and blue blazer, with long blue stockings. Dress regulations were relaxed a little on Sundays. It was then that tweed jacket and grey flannels were donned. Boy coming from Scottish homes have a fondness for wearing the kilt.

Sedbergh has been staunchly "Yorksher". When a choir from the town took part in a choral competition held at Kirkby Lonsdale in the 1920s, Sir Henry Wood listened to a large number of choirs. After the Sedbergh choir had sung, Sir Henry (who did not appreciate that there were choirs other than from Westmorland) observed: These people are not from Westmorland; they are from Yorkshire. You can hear it in their voices."

Sedbergh was noted for its personalities. Freda M Kay (subsequently Freda Trot, who died in January, 2008, aged 88) once reminded the readers of *The Dalesman* of Old Sebber in well-researched articles. Mally Gibson, one of the outstanding nineteenth century characters, was noted for her hand-knitting. This was not to wile away the time. Knitting was a prime way of augmeting local

The main street of Sedbergh, once unfairly described as being "half dead for most of the time and fully dead on Thursday, when the shops close early"!

incomes.

Mally was dour, grim, stern with the struggle to make a living. She would emerge, complete with stool, from her low, dark cottage in a clustered yard and make her way to a place where she might keep her eye on "t'goin's on" while her wooden needles flew in and out, her balls of "bump" lessening as her garment grew. By knitting unceasingly the whole day, Mally might earn twopence-halfpenny. The "Bump Master" came from Kendal fortnightly, bringing a new supply of gaily-coloured yarn and collecting the finished goods. Mally therefore put a linen strip on her weak wrist and rattled away to add her share to Sedbergh's export trade.

Dent, a few miles from Sedbergh, became noted for its knitters because of the publicity given to their activities by Southey in his novel called *The Doctor*. He coined what became a memorable expression: "Terrible knitters 'e Dent." Hereabouts, a knitter of "bump" [coarsely-spun wool] rocked backwards and forwards (also crooning a song) as her nimble fingers handled the four curved metal needles. One needle was slipped into a hole at the end of a dagger-like knitting stick (known in other areas as a sheath), which was held firm by a leather belt. William Howitt (1844) wrote of Dent knitters who sat "rocking to and fro like so many weird wizards. They burn no candle but knit by the light of the peat fire.

And this rocking motion is connected with a mode of knitting peculiar to the place, called swaying..."

A familiar figure on market days recalled by Freda Kay (who became Freda Trot) was Egg Alice. She sallied forth in her red garribaldi [a short coat] to sell her eggs, fowls and, in season, her plums. Alice lived alone on the foot of Baugh Fell for thirty years, her hens and ducks sharing the sod-house which was of her own making. Later, Alice employed a man to build her a two-roomed house of stone. She carried the stones from a nearby beck. As Freda wrote, half a century ago, the outline might still be seen on the bleak fell near Sedbergh; it was surrounded by her storm-broken plum trees.

The Howgills, these slate mountains, have their old Silurian rocks exposed in grand style at Cautley Crags, which rise 2,000-ft above the valley bottom. Here, too, Red Gill Beck descends over 600-ft in a series of cascades to form Cautley Spout. It is reached easily from The Calf and this route provides an exhilarating round trip from Sedbergh.

You cannot see The Calf from the town. It shows itself at Calders, less than a half-mile from the summit. The summit is disappointing. It is an almost insignificant mound among a range of high, rounded fells. You might look for a higher peak but there is none. The panorama of Lakeland hills, of Whernside, Ingleborough and Penyghent, also the fells to the east and the coastline to the west may be studied at an equal advantage during the ascent.

With regard to the Howgills, Ian Plant, who died tragically through drowing when exploring flooded passages in a pothole called Bull Pot of the Witches, was impressed by the fortitude of Rough Fell sheep and wrote: "Even on The Calf, at 2,220ft above sea level, they are unperturbed by the wind which rips up the valleys to the west." The Rough Fells, he added, are unprotected by walls or fences. "There are unlimited grazing rights on the open fells – fells that are dissected by deep ravines and lively watercourses. Sheep tracks vanish overnight in foul weather, becoming part of the scree which litters their slopes. Stream beds are a jumble of boulders of all shapes and sizes."

The farmer at High Hill Farm told Ian it was difficult country even for the fittest sheepdog. "The dogs soon get tired and so do I. I've been part way up there on a tractor but it's very dicey. We had some sheep fast on rocks in Hobdale Gill one snowtime. We had to make a track and find a leader among the flock that would lead the rest of the sheep out...We don't lose much stock, though, despite the unrestricted grazing rights on the open fells, where mingling is bound to occur. There are three sheep meetings a year and strays are always returned with other

Exterior and interior views of Brigflatts, the Quaker Meeting House near Sedbergh.

flocks." (High Hill Farm is now derelict).

On the last occasion when I climbed to the highspots of the Howgills, it was market day in Sedbergh and streets were thronged by slowly-moving vehicles and briskly chatting people. I strode along the main street, passed the overspill part of the market and found a typical north-country sign: "To the Fell". It was short and to the point. A notice on a five-barred gate announced it was lambing time and urged visitors to keep their dogs under control.

Faded foxgloves looked like spent fireworks. A tall mast bristled with bars, some doubtless for mobile phones, which most people now carry. I broke free of walls and began a steady climb on a path between tousled vegetation, with a fell rising at 45 degrees to my left and descending at 45 degrees to where a beck was gurgling to itself. A raven croaked as it crossed an otherwise empty sky. Rough Fells – the sheep breed that speckles the Howgills, had dark faces relieved by frontal patches of white.

Walker on the Howgill Fells, heading for the 2,220ft summit of The Calf.

I was en route for The Calf, the attic of the Howgills and it was here that I became aware of the wind. It had been of moderate strength but now it was chillingly more intrusive, with gusts that made me sway in my boots. I donned an anorak, clutched my walking sticks until my hands drained of blood, and resigned myself to its constant company as I entered the Howgill big-dipper.

In this curvaceous landscape – this area of huge humps and deep hollows – the path had an aversion to being level. The hill slopes were pock-marked by deep scrapes in which sheep would shelter from the most pitiful winds or from snow. Glancing to my right, I beheld a wonderland of fell and dale, with the sunlight breaking through light mist. In the distance were dove-grey outlines of familiar hills – Gragareth, Ingleborough, Whernside.

The wind had grounded most birds but a buzzard circled, crows swirled in the turbulent air and, astonishingly, there were swallows in flight. I surmounted two impressive slopes on my way to The Calf, its summit – and that of the Howgills – marked by a triangulation pillar – and nothing else. I had found a suitable place; I might eat my sandwiches in the lee of Calders. On the way back, the wind was so loud I could hear nothing else. The effects of the wind lessened during the descent and I walked for a time in sunlight on ground that was speckled with the little yellow flower called tormentil.

The National Trust has preserved the Temperance Hotel, a clean, whitewashed building by the roadside that has a little farm with fell rights to the Howgills. The hotel was built as the Cross Keys coaching inn in 1732 and remained licensed until the early part of the century, when it was purchased by someone with strong views about temperance. It was sold to the National Trust on condition that it would never again be used as a public house.

4 – BESIDE MORECAMBE BAY

Hannah has grown to love the area where landscape meets a seascape in the vicinity of Grange-over-Sands. The landscape, historically Furness, lies north of Morecambe Bay. The dominant geological feature is the younger bluey-grey strata of the Silurian series, evident in an area from about Windermere to Cartmel. It may lack the gee-whiz element of the volcanic rocks at the heart of the district but this gentler landscape has the appeal of little fields and woodland of the deciduous variety, rather than of conifers set in well-organised ranks.

The seascape is sea for only part of the day for this is Morecambe Bay, a massive inlet. The tide races across this sodden desert with the speed of a good horse. It holds no fears for Hannah for her special friends in the area are Cedric Robinson, the Sands Guide, and his wife. Their ancient home – which goes with the job of Sands Guide - overlooks a railway that rims the Bay and keeps its shoreline stable. Beyond the tracks are the restless tides, about the whims of which Cedric is the undoubted authority.

A M Wakefield, a lady with a profound knowledge of the area, wrote in 1909: "Whence comes the fascination of Morecambe Bay? Is it from the dangerous excitement surrounding the 'shifting sands', with their ever-increasing death-toll; or from the changing channels, in which often even a week's time finds substantial alteration; or from the silent creep of the 'bore' wave that has swept in too swiftly and silently for many a traveller?" She mentioned the mutability of the sands and their associations as exercising a great attraction, adapting themselves to every change of mood.

To Morecambe Bay, in distant times, came waves of settlers, traders and adventurers. It is believed that the main Roman invasion army under the military governor, Gnaeus Julius Agricola, entered the region by the coastal route in the autumn of 79 AD. It was the Norsefolk who left the most abiding evidence of their colonisation. Dr Fred Hogarth, who was a medical practitioner at Morecambe and knew the Bay extremely well, believed that the curious duplication of the vowel sound in local names denotes their old Norse origin. There is skeer for a patch of rough sea bed; roost for a tidal-rip or drop-off; craam or kraam, an iron rake with a long wooden shaft used for collecting mussels and haaf, which is a hand-net with which salmon and sea trout were caught.

Morecambe Bay and the estuaries of rivers that flow into it have been the subject of much speculative prose. You might, for example, forecast the weather by walking on the sands and sniffing. This was written in the 18th century by one John Lucas. He asserted that "whoever walks upon these Sands [of the Kent estuary] a little before Rain will hear a hissing Noise, occasioned by the breathing of innumerable little Bibbles, and will feel a noysom stinking Savour; the Reason of which I take to be, that the Pores of the Sand as well as of the Earth, are at such times unlock'd, and so streams of crude sulphur with a mixture of Salts do breath forth and occasion this ungrateful Smell. This the neighbouring inhabitants take for as sure a Prognastik of Rain."

For centuries, crossing the Sands from Hest Bank to Kents Bank was more direct, less tedious, than rough roads on the mainland for travellers heading for Furness and West Cumberland. The Sands way did not, unlike normal roads, need any attention. Each new tide swept it clean, removing all traces of feet and hooves and wheels of those who had crossed. Among the drawbacks were the varying times when crossing was possible and the presence of river channels and quicksands. Lake Poets like Wordsworth revelled in the Oversands route. There was nothing like a spell in the wilderness to prepare the mind for the grandeur of the Lake District.

A sands guide, once known as carter, had a stressful job. Consider the work done by John Carter, who petitioned for a wage increase in 1715. The petitioner's father was carter before him "and had patent and salary paid him." He was allowed to augment his income by selling ale in his house excise free. The petitioner was obliged for his wok as guide to "keep two horses, summer and winter."

He had to "attend the edy four miles upon the sands, twelve hours in every twenty-four hours." His horses, often in water, were starved with cold and so often thrown into distemper that the cost of keeping them was great. The petitioner "undergoes great hardships by his being exposed to the wind and cold upon the plain sands, and being often wet, and he by seeking our new fords every variation of the edy, and upon happenings in fogs and mists, often put in danger of his life."

John Wesley, burning with evangelical zeal and therefore impatient of delay on his journey, arrived at the edge of Morecambe Bay in 1759. He crossed the sands to reach West Cumberland but there were unhandy tidal flows. He later suggested that it was often quicker to go round by Kendal and Keswick on the journey to the Cumberland coast.

This is a young landscape. Morecambe Bay has outcropping rocks that are the remains of moraines of boulder clay left by the glaciers of the Ice Ages that littered the area with boulders from other regions – with greenstone from the Lake District and with red granite from Shap. Apart from using the Bay as a part-time highway, industry thrived. By the 18th century a shipping trade connected the Furness coastline with the ports of Wales and the Severn. An ebb tide bared the beds of cockles and mussels, bringing local people on to the Bay with baskets and carts.

Flookburgh was the village tuned to fishing. It was of the horse-and-cart variety and the net is now towed by a tractor. Trawling for shrimps in the channels at low tide kept the community economically happy. A purse net is used. It has an extended tail, into which the shrimps are directed. The mouth of the trawl is a foot-wide gap between beams. The shrimp industry is based on the knowledge that a shrimp jumps if it is startled!

When Flookburgh men go cockling, they have an appliance christened Jumbo. A local man, Peter Butler, invited this device, which consists of a broad base board with long handles. With its aid, the sand can be agitated, coaxing the cockles to the surface, where they are scooped up with a fork-like object known as a kraam.

A popular walk from Grange-over-Sands takes in Hampsfell Hospice, which is set on a limestone plateau and is the most outstanding viewpoint in the district. I strode into Grange, mindful that its name relates to a granary or outlying farm connected with a religious house, in this case Furness Abbey. The suffix "over-Sands" was bestowed in Victorian times, when the place was becoming touristy. It was to distinguish the place from other Granges – and, perhaps, to divert attention from the muddy nature of the shoreline, where the River Kent – the fastest river in England – left a murky tidemark.

Grange grew remarkably during the latter part of the 19th century. A church was established in 1853, the first incumbent being the Rev Mr Rigg, who travelled by coach. Entering the Kent channel, the coach settled in soft mud. The horses were removed and outside passengers scrambled off. Then someone remembered the parson. He was not in the best of health and as he sat inside the coach he was swaddled in clothing and rugs, hardly aware of what was going on.

The doors of the coach could not be opened, the lower part being already under sand level. Mr Rigg was hauled through an open window and ushered to the shore. He left behind in the coach a valise containing valuable documents connected with the new church. His ministry thus had a disappointing start. The months went by. Then the tide delivered the battered coach to Holme Island. Inside was the valise. The church documents were intact.

Four years after the church was built came the arrival of the Furness Railway, which stabilised the coast. High tides had surged as far as the main street. Navvies fulfilled with great efficiency the Canute-like aspiration of holding back the sea. Walk around the ornamental gardens and you are on what was once the beach. The railway gave quick access and egress to tourists, some of whom were later to arrive by boat in a service that connected Morecambe with a jetty at Grange.

In Grange, I passed the row of cafes and souvenir shops, complete with Victorian iron verandas, that overlook those ornamental gardens, as a duck-haunted ornamental lake which the poet Norman Nicholson described as being "of almost excruciating prettiness". My walk to Hampsfell might be said to have begun in Grange when I turned off the pavement on to a path that led me into a tract of woodland where small birds were tuning up for their spring chorus.

Paths abounded. They lay between limestone outcrops and trees in a woodscape lagged with moss. I walked quietly. The deciduous woods in this area are the haunt of roe deer. I heard a gruff bark - the call of a disgruntled roebuck. Eventually I stood on a lip of limestone and beheld, far below, an assembly of large houses lying beside the Cartmel road. I recognised Charney Road, where Harry J Scott, founder of *The Dalesman* magazine, and his wife Dorothy, lived in their later years. The view was much more extensive, taking in the expanse of coarse grass that has formed between the promenade at Grange and the Bay.

Also in view was Humphrey Head, one of very few sea cliffs along the Lancashire coast. The shoreline is so low that the Headland seems much higher than its 160-ft. Surfaced roads lead to it, ending abruptly at high tide mark. Use the road system, and the level crossing associated with the Furness line, and you may notice Wraysholme Tower, once a castle, now a farmhouse, with pele tower adjoining. Here lived the Harrington family at a time when a wolf was to be found in the area. The last wolf in England, it is said, tongue in cheek. From Humphrey Head, look across the bay to the blocky form of the Heysham atomic power station.

Clearing the area where houses clung to a hillside, I entered farmland, noticing that one of the fields held an impressive but disused limekiln. My destination was the road at Spring Bank Cottage, from which I had a short path to negotiate before reaching the main road. The byroad was flanked by walls and hedges, liberally covered with ivy, from which dangled bunches of black berries.

A step-stile marked Cartmel took me on to the Grange Fell golf course, offering a splendid view of the Coniston Fells, sprinkled with snow, and the Vale of Cartmel. The old parish of Cartmel, sixty square miles in extent, is almost surrounded by water. To the north lies Windermere – the lake, not the town named after it – overflowing as the River Leven, which is the westward border between Cartmel and Furness. On the east flows the River Winster. Miles of Cartmel's southern boundary are tide-washed. Cartmel has its own little watercourse, the Ea

Hampsfell Hospice, the most outstanding viewpoint in the Grange-over-Sands district.

[an ancient word for "water"].

The first thing to remember about Cartmel is that up to the time of the Romantic Movement – roughly the middle of the 18th century – the place was probably the most isolated part of England. At the end of the 7th century, the King of Northumbria (Egfrith) gave the lands of Cartmel "with all the Britons therein" to St Cuthbert, Bishop of Lindisfarne. He ordered that a Priory should be built between two springs, each flowing in a different direction – conditions that were found at the site of modern Cartmel.

So the village is dominated, as it had been for centuries, by a Priory – more precisely, the Priory Church of St Mary and St Michael - notable for the unusual diagonal extension to its blocky central tower. It was a cosy situation, flanked by Bigland Heights (west) and Hampsfield Fell, now Hampsfell (right). Gordon Bottomley introduced his poem "New Year's Eve 1913" with the heart-stirring words:

> *O, Cartmel bells ring soft tonight*
> *And Cartmel bells ring clear,*
> *But I lie far away tonight,*
> *Listening with my dear...*

I reached the village by keeping close to the side of a busy road. Cartmel village is familiar to Hannah, who has doubtless admired the magnificent Priory and Gatehouse while on her way to the little, beckside Methodist chapel where she has spoken of her life and interests. Cartmel Priory, like other important religious houses, has had its ups and downs. An "up" in the twelfth century occurred when William Marshall, Earl of Pembroke, gathered at Cartmel a community of Canons Regular of St Augustus.

The major "down" was when Henry VIII dissolved the monasteries in 1537, Cartmel being counted as one of the "lesser monasteries". The Priory buildings were looted, but the people claimed parochial rights and were allowed to keep a part of the building for worship. The south aisle of the chancel is known as the Town Choir to this day. An "up" in the Cartmel story was saving that aisle. It led to the restoration of the whole building by George Preston, of Holker Hall, whose practical help was offered in 1618. He adorned the chancel "with curious carved woodwork."

In the churchyard are sobering reminders of the old days. One family lost all five children for various reasons before any of them had reached the age of ten. Inside the Priory is a flagstone marking the last resting place of a man who had been overswept by the tide while on the Bay.

The road I now followed was beside Cartmel's celebrated racecourse. In due course I was across the road, on a Public Bridleway, crossing fields and a footbridge made of new planks that spanned what appeared on the map as Mucky Beck. Eventually I reached a bridge in the corner of a field; the bridge was composed of two pieces of slate.

During my walk towards Hampsfell (the fell of a Norseman named Hamr), I followed a drive to Longlands, a Jane Austen type of house set in a valley where fields were neatly laid out, where the boundary of what might have been a deer park was flanked by ultra-wide hedges and a tall wall, and where a walled garden of great size was still very much in use. On the hillside was a folly – a battlemented tower of little use beyond being a point of observation.

The track I used to climb Hampsfell bore the trackmarks of motor vehicles. The hillside was littered with gorse bushes. A quartet of chattering magpies gave the scene a sense of life. The view was magnificent, taking in the whole Vale of Cartmel, the shores of Morecambe Bay and, spread grandly across the northern skyline, a backdrop of snow-crested Lakeland fells.

Now an area of limestone outcrops was lit up dramatically by a waning sun. The Hospice retained its glory as one of the finest vantage points in the Lake

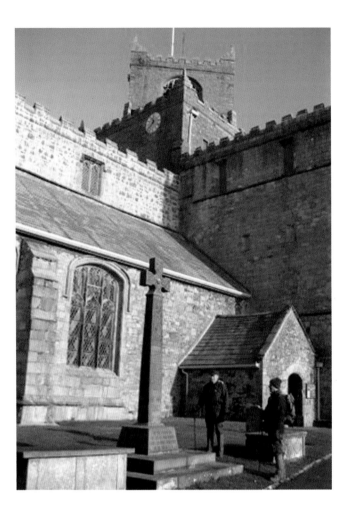

Cartmel Priory boasts an extraordinary diagonal extension to its central tower.

Counties, offering a panoramic view that might be enjoyed in detail using a direction indicator set on top. The rim of the indicator was marked with degrees of a compass, so that a visitor might refer to a list and then, turning the pointer to the degree required, looking along it to observe objects of interest, such as Chapel, Island, in the Leven Estuary, Dunmail Raise or the Langdale Pikes. The inner walls of the hospice feature boards on which are given details of the structure.

The descent to Grange included a tract of Egglerslack Wood (a jay screeched). One of the Grange cafes provided me with the customary tea and toasted teacakes.

EPILOGUE

Hannah's life in the dale-country has spanned a social revolution. She was brought up in the tidy austerity of a dale-country farmhouse – and, at the age of forty-eight, being guest of honour at the Women of the Year lunch at the Savoy in London, she spent the night in a luxurious riverside suite. Much of her life has been bounded by ranges of fells and not knowing much about what lay beyond.

She is no fashion-plate, remarking to a visiting city journalist that as a girl she was told: "If you have anything better, you must get it off and don your old things." Hannah liked trousers, which are "handy and comfortable." She was not too proud to accept second-hand clothes from friends. She was usually late for appointments, not because she dawdled. It was just that she didn't like rushing! "If I have to hurry, everything goes wrong." She followed the guidance of a familiar ditty: "I eat when I'm hungry; I drink when I'm dry." She ate slowly. There was nothing elaborate for breakfast, just toast, the slices of bread hacked from the loaf. Ready-sliced bread was beyond her reach.

Celebrity resulting from the film *Too Long a Winter* opened up the world to her. She trotted round a quarter of the globe, but retained her special love for the homeland. She preferred meeting people and action to simply gazing at landscape. It was exciting for her when, as a friend of Cedric Robinson, Guide to the Sands of Morecambe Bay, she was taken part way across a bird-busy bay. (She was a little queasy at first, thinking about quicksands!)

*Opposite and over: Two contrasting images of Hannah
– on and off the farm.*

Social changes in the Dales began to be noticed in the mid-1930s with an improvement in roads and transport, making an area like Baldersdale less reliant on its own resources. It saw the decline of some of the rural craftsmen. Hannah remembered when a local farmer might keep cattle, sheep, pigs, hens and geese. (In her childhood, it was not unusual to see a flock of geese being driven along a road.) When sheep were being clipped, friends helped each other in a voluntary rota, the clipping day at a farm including plenty to eat and drink. There might also be a dance in the evening.

Hannah was quite fond of looking at sheep; offered a black-faced lamb as a gift, she called it Nanny Bateson. She did not care much for handling sheep. "I never liked doing the clipping." The bales of wool were collected and taken to the urban mills to be converted into cloth. Some of the wool came back in the form of grey blankets, which were for sale. Pig-killing took place when there was R in the month. (The warmer months were avoided). She had happy times with pigs, but found the pig-killing depressing. Only the squeal was wasted. Pig blood was made into black puddings. Hannah helped to make sausages. Flitches hanged from hooks in the kitchen or living room ceiling.

Despite her rather primitive way of life – a consequence of farming in isolation without help – there was about Hannah a quiet dignity and undoubted charm. When I met her there was no risk of running out of topics to discuss, almost all of these connected with farming. The only truly sad note was at the thought of the coming winter. Outside, sunlight brought a responsive glow from the tawny ground. Patches of rushes arched their backs against the wind. Curlews had drifted away, but there were some Canada geese on the reservoir. Her garden showed the full summer flush of growth, with especially fine specimens of nettle.

Hannah's face clouded over as she spoke of her unending winter routine, when she entered her house simply to eat and to sleep. Hers was an exceptional case, but even on farms where there are several workers, the prolonged winter has its affect, with weary-looking faces and flat voices. The Pennine winter was, to Hannah, too long for comfort. As she sat and knitted, or just sat, she thought of the good times. The hair is soft, whiter as snow, drawn back from a face that is smooth and pink. There's an inner glow of serenity as she remembers times long gone, when her mother bustled about the house and uncle was always ready for a chat.

Hannah once described herself as "a one-woman farmer in a small way. It doesn't allow you to do a lot of things that should be done. Things you would like to do." Life at the farm had not been easy. She was always pleased to hear the

The Teesdale Hills – with their
'winding streams and mountains steep'.

curlew; its fluty calls indicated that spring would come sooner or later, sometimes later, but it would come. Hannah, in later life, felt she had been lucky to find good homes for her livestock. Cotherstone, her retirement village, suited her, being surrounded by nice scenery.

She contrives to get to the chapel on a Sunday. A Methodist minister friend who recently took over a service at the request of a colleague in the Teesdale circuit was pleased to see Hannah in the congregation. The last time Freda and I met her was at the cottage in Cotherstone. She had a washer and spin-drier which were as delivered. Hannah had not got round to using them. In any case, she liked to do her washing by hand, using a bucket and plunger. She used a friend's washing line and laid the heavier clothes – overcoat and the like – on another friend's field if there was any warmth in the sun.

We reminisced. When the time for departure came, Hannah waved us off. She was clad in second-best clothes. There were wellingtons on her feet. The wave was similar to the one when we first met her, then left after an enjoyable chat. A wave that began as we left her and continued until we were out of sight.

Visiting journalists were enchanted by the way she summed up her likes and dislikes; her feelings about the old life. Alec Donaldson, the first man to tell the world about Hannah, concluded his article thus: "You may wish to salute, as I do, the Lonely Lady of Low Birk Hatt – remote and independent but quietly content in her upland place far from a world she tends to ignore." Hannah does not like to brood on the old days. Her heart aches when she recalls Rosa, her favourite cow. To go back would upset her. Her life at Low Birk Hatt was "better felt than explained".

Hannah describes herself as a very ordinary person. "I am just me." I asked her if she had a New Year resolution. No – she had not got one. "If I had, I would only break it. My plans always go awry." Hannah, a great sentimentalist, closed a chapter of one her books with a poem from the pen of Richard Watson (1833-1891). He called it "The Teesdale Hills":

I've wandered many a weary mile,
And in strange countries been,
I've dwelt in towns and on wild moors
And curious sights I've seen;
But still my heart clings to the dale,
Where Tees rolls to the sea,
Compared with what I've seen I'll say,
The Teesdale hills for me.

Let minstrels sing till they are hoarse
of Scotia's woods and dells,
And winding streams and mountains steep,
Where bloom sweet heather bells,
Their strains still fail to touch my heart,
My fav'rite ones shall be
Those that remind me of my home -
The Teesdale hills for me.

TRUEMAN'S TALES

'Fiery Fred' – Yorkshire's Cricketing Giant

By John Morgan and David Joy

With contributions from: Dickie Bird, Ian Botham, Geoffrey Boycott, Brian Close, Raymond Illingworth, Bill Pertwee and Harvey Smith.

This book began as a collaboration between Fred Trueman and David Joy in early 2006. Then came Fred's untimely death. Sports journalist, and long-time friend of Fred Trueman, John Morgan, completed the book, which became a fitting tribute to a cricketing legend.
Fully illustrated. Hardback.

BETWEEN THE TIDES

The Perilous Beauty of Morecambe Bay

By Cedric Robinson

Foreword by HRH The Duke of Edinburgh

Cedric Robinson records his 45 years as Queen's Guide to the Sands, an historic role that stretches back many centuries. In this book, Cedric describes the guided walk across Morecambe Bay, the wildlife encountered there and past tragedies on these treacherous sands. Superb colour photographs depict the Bay in all its amazing variety.
Fully illustrated. Hardback.

GREAT YORKSHIRE

A Celebration of 150 Shows

Foreword by HRH The Price of Wales

Published to mark the 150th Great Yorkshire Show in July 2008, this book celebrates a unique institution. Lavishly illustrated with archive photographs from the Yorkshire Agricultural Society and the Yorkshire Post. This large format, full colour hardback is a book to treasure.

STORM FORCE

Britain's Wildest Weather

TV weathermen Michael Fish MBE, Ian McCaskill and Paul Hudson recall the most devastating gales and ferocious floods in Britain's history

Storm Force is full of fascinating facts, extraordinary human stories, by turns amusing, inspiring, astonishing and downright weird! Beautifully produced in hardback, this is a book with many dramatic photographs that also provides an exciting read and is at the same time immensely thought provoking.

FROZEN IN TIME

The Years When Britain Shivered

Ian McCaskill and Paul Hudson remember when winters really were winters.

Using dramatic pictures and news reports from national and regional archives, recalling the worst winters ever with particular attention given to 1947, 1963 and 1979. An exciting and thought provoking read.
Fully illustrated. Hardback.

Visit www.greatnorthernbooks.co.uk

Also by Great Northern Books

ESSENCE OF THE YORKSHIRE COAST

By Malcolm Barker

A beautifully illustrated book, featuring recently discovered archive photography.

This book goes behind the scenery to look in depth at life and work along the coast. It puts a new perspective on such subjects as fishing, smuggling, shipping and shipwrecks, and the proud story of lifeboats putting to sea in conditions of dire peril. It focuses on communities large and small, ranging from trawling out of Hull to the traditional fishing village of Staithes, and from Scarborough in its heyday to life at remote Spurn Point.
Fully illustrated. Hardback.

ESSENCE OF WHITBY

By Malcolm Barker

A superbly researched and beautifully illustrated book that looks in depth at the history of this popular seaside town. Glorious photographs enhance Malcolm Barker's illuminating, informative text.
Fully illustrated. Hardback.

MOUSEMAN

The Legacy of Robert Thompson of Kilburn

By Patricia Lennon and David Joy

This new book incorporates a history of Robert (Mousey) Thompson, a guide to some of his most famous pieces of furniture across the UK and information on how to identify and date Mouseman furniture.
A beautiful, hardback, large format, full colour book.

YORKSHIRE IN PARTICULAR

An Alternative A-Z

Edited by Michael Hickling

Foreword by Gervase Phinn

Asked to 'spell out' the essence of Yorkshire, journalists on the county's leading newspaper, The Yorkshire Post, have gathered together a diverse selection of people, places, products and peculiarities. The result is a book that will be treasured by all who have a special affection for this fascinating region.
Fully illustrated. Hardback.

A YEAR OF FAMILY RECIPES

by Lesley Wild

Customers at Bettys and Bettys Cookery School have been asking for a cookery book for years. A Year of Family Recipes is a personal collection of over 100 recipes by Lesley Wild from the Bettys family.
This 260 page hardbacked book covers everything from bread and jam making to suppers and salads; home baking and sophisticated entertaining.
Stunning photographs. Hardback.

Visit www.greatnorthernbooks.co.uk